ECLECTIC ENGLISH CLASSICS

MACAULAY'S

LAYS OF ANCIENT ROME

AND

OTHER POEMS

EDITED BY

W. PATTERSON ATKINSON, A. M.

ENGLISH DEPARTMENT, JERSEY CITY HIGH SCHOOL

NEW YORK ·:· CINCINNATI ·:· CHICAGO
AMERICAN BOOK COMPANY

Copyright, 1913, by
AMERICAN BOOK COMPANY

MACAULAY'S LAYS
W. P. I

In the interest of creating a more extensive selection of rare historical book reprints, we have chosen to reproduce this title even though it may possibly have occasional imperfections such as missing and blurred pages, missing text, poor pictures, markings, dark backgrounds and other reproduction issues beyond our control. Because this work is culturally important, we have made it available as a part of our commitment to protecting, preserving and promoting the world's literature. Thank you for your understanding.

CONTENTS

	PAGE
INTRODUCTION	
Life of Macaulay	7
Characteristics	12
Writings	14
Style	18
Place and service	19
Chronological Table	20
List of Essays	21
References	22
Outline of Macaulay's Preface to *Lays*	22
Legends underlying the *Lays*	24
MAP	26
HORATIUS	27
THE BATTLE OF THE LAKE REGILLUS	49
VIRGINIA	76
THE PROPHECY OF CAPYS	90
IVRY	103
THE BATTLE OF NASEBY	106
THE ARMADA	109
NOTES	113

INTRODUCTION

I. LIFE

THOMAS BABINGTON MACAULAY, who later became Lord Macaulay, was born in the house of his uncle, Thomas Babington, at Rothley Temple, Leicestershire, England, October 25th, 1800. He came of serious-minded people. His father, Zachary Macaulay, was an upright, stern, religious Scotchman, who devoted his life to the abolition of negro slavery in the British possessions. His mother, Selina Mills, was the daughter of a member of the Society of Friends (Quakers) in Bristol, while his ancestors on his father's side were for several generations Scotch Presbyterian ministers.

Macaulay was a precocious child, displaying at a surprisingly early age a wonderful memory, an unusual facility in composition, both oral and written, and a passion for reading. These traits, in some of which he is resembled by a later eminent Scotch literary man, Robert Louis Stevenson, were dominant throughout his life. His habit of reading began about the age of three; he wrote long compositions in prose and in verse before he was eight; and his memory was prodigious from the earliest. This precocity was doubtless fostered by intimate and early contact with the eminent men associated with his father.

His education began very young as a day scholar at a school in Clapham, a suburb of London, where his family resided. Soon having outgrown its possibilities he was sent to the boarding school of the Rev. Mr. Preston, at Little Shelford, near Cambridge. Here before he was thirteen he was translating Xenophon and the *Odyssey* from Greek, composing Latin verses and reading Vergil, writing compositions in English, engaging in debates, reading French for his own amusement, and studying geometry. Though he was precocious as a young child, his studies at Mr. Preston's school are no proof of exceptional ability; they formed the ordinary work of boys of his age. In those days Greek and Latin were studied for many more years than they are now in this country and consequently the pupils really mastered both languages.

In Mr. Preston's school Macaulay had been in a Cambridge atmosphere, so by a natural transition in October, 1818, in the beginning of his nineteenth year, he entered Trinity College, Cambridge, of which College his old master was an ex-Fellow. Here he twice took the Chancellor's medal for composition in English verse, and, besides other prizes, won in 1821 the Craven Scholarship for excellence in the classics. He crowned his University career by winning a Fellowship of Trinity College by examination in 1824, whereby he became for seven years one of sixty masters of that institution, sharing in its privileges and revenues, though not residing there. He enjoyed his college course of six years to the full, taking part in its social life with zest and finding pleasure in all his studies except mathematics. Among his companions he was famous as a talker.

In 1825, while yet in his twenty-fifth year, there was published in the August number of *The Edinburgh Review* his essay on Milton. It was received with extraordinary favor. His style was admired and heartily commended, by none so much as by Jeffrey, the editor. But this was not the first time that his writings had appeared in print. Two years before he had written a number of articles for Knight's *Quarterly Magazine,* contributions which had doubtless led to the invitation to send articles to *The Edinburgh.* From this time, with occasional interruptions due to holding office, he wrote till his death, contributing to the *Review* alone till 1844.

The money gained from literature was very acceptable as his father had failed in business and the son had become the main ıpport of the family which included many brothers and sisters. ving to Zachary Macaulay's absorption in the antislavery crusade the family fortunes had been declining for several years so that in 1823, while yet at Cambridge, Macaulay was glad to take private pupils. Now he took up the study of law, with no great relish it is true, as was the case with Stevenson, but although called to the bar in 1826 he achieved no success as a lawyer. His writing combined with his fellowship kept things going but it was fortunate that in 1828 he was appointed a Commissioner of Bankruptcy. These three sources brought his income to about $5,000 a year. This appointment is an evidence of his prominence and of his recognized ability, for it came unsought.

Another unsought honor was the offer of a seat in Parliament for the borough of Calne, made by Lord Lansdowne who did not know him personally but who was struck by the forcible articles in *The Review*. This offer was possible because at that time many localities represented in Parliament were so small as to be owned absolutely by one person who could dictate the candidate to be elected. Sometimes these places had no population at all, for instance Old Sarum. Such places were called "pocket boroughs."[1] This selection was most agreeable to Macaulay who took a great interest in politics. It led also to another success, for his speeches in Parliament were triumphs of oratory.

But members of Parliament at that time were not paid. Further, in 1831 a bill was passed to reform the bankruptcy practice, for which Macaulay voted though it abolished his office. Then for a time he was so poor that he had to sell his Cambridge medals despite the fact that he was a foremost man in Parliament and a welcome guest in the best houses in London. As a reward for his hard work in support of the Reform Bill of 1832, a measure which greatly improved the whole English electoral system, he was appointed a Commissioner of the Board of Control, a body which represented the crown in its relation to the East India Company, that group of men who

[1] Consult McCarthy's *The Epoch of Reform*, pp. 25-26.

governed India. Shortly afterward he became the Board's secretary.

The Reform Bill of 1832 gave to Leeds, an important manufacturing city, two representatives in Parliament. The Whig Party, of which he was a member, asked Macaulay to be its candidate, and though he could have been reëlected without trouble for Calne, he felt it his duty to his party to agree. In the campaign he asserted his independence by refusing to pledge his future actions in Parliament; and in spite of loud remonstrances against this policy, he carried the election.

The year 1834 is an important date in Macaulay's life for it was at that time that he went to India as the Legal Adviser to the Supreme Council of that land. He gave up his parliamentary career because from the salary of his new office, £10,000 a year, he would be able at the expiration of his term to have saved sufficient money to make him independent and able to provide for his family. It was a sacrifice but he gladly made it. On the outward voyage to his new post, which took nearly four months in a sailing vessel, he devoted himself to reading, covering an enormous number of books chiefly in Latin and in Greek. In India he did great service. Besides his regular duties he was a member of two very important committees, one of which drew up the Indian Penal Code, a compilation that has evoked the enthusiastic admiration of the legal profession, the other of which prepared and put into operation an entirely new system of education. It is pleasant to add that his sister Hannah accompanied him, for his family was as much devoted to him as he was to them. In the strange country she met and married Mr. Trevelyan. Their son, years afterward, wrote the standard biography of his famous uncle.

Macaulay returned to England in 1838 a free man, free from office and free from the worry over money. For a short time he gave himself to the enjoyment of literature and of travel, in the same year making a tour of Italy. But his leisure was not for long. In 1839 he became a member of Parliament for Edinburgh and in the same year joined the Cabinet as the Secretary at War. He plunged into the new work with characteristic vigor, at the same time writing some of his most famous essays. He held office till a change of ministry occurred in 1841 when he was reëlected for Edinburgh.

Again Macaulay had time for writing. During the period from 1841 to 1846 he wrote seven articles for *The Review*, issued *The Lays of Ancient Rome*, and prepared a collected edition of his essays. Then once more, his party having sought his services, he became a Cabinet minister as Paymaster-general. But another change of ministry soon occurred and in the general election of 1847 Macaulay was defeated at Edinburgh. This defeat was due to the great unrest in Scotland in matters pertaining to politics and to religion, and to discontent with Macaulay's independence.

His leisure once more regained, Macaulay turned his thought seriously to a long occupation, one which held him to the end of his life, his *History of England*. Honors began to come to him. In February, 1847, he became a Trustee of the British Museum, in 1849 Lord Rector of Glasgow University, and Fellow of the Royal Society. In 1852 he was also reëlected a member of Parliament for Edinburgh, which being unsought and occurring without effort on his part, is to be counted an honor and an act of reparation. His seat, however, he resigned in 1856.

In 1852 Macaulay became for the first time in his life seriously ill. His heart was affected and until his death he was at no time a well man. But he enjoyed life, writing faithfully and with love for his work. More honors came. He was made a Foreign Member of the French Academy, a member of the Prussian Order of Merit, High Steward of Cambridge, and in 1854 Oxford conferred upon him the degree of D. C. L. But the greatest honor was his elevation in 1857 to the Peerage as Baron Macaulay of Rothley.

His life now rapidly drew to a close. After having apartments in the Albany for many years, he settled down in 1856 at

Holly Lodge, Kensington, a suburb of London. Holly Lodge was a villa standing by itself, screened from view by dense foliage, and presenting a rural appearance. Here surrounded by books, interested for the first time in a garden, watched over by loving friends and relatives, he passed the last three years of his life. And here December 28, 1859, he quietly passed away. On January 9, 1860, he was reverently laid to rest in Westminster Abbey.

II. CHARACTERISTICS

In reference to Macaulay's appearance it was once written: "There came up a short manly figure, marvelously upright, with a bad neckcloth, and one hand in his waistcoat pocket. Of regular beauty he had little to boast; but in faces where there is an expression of great power, or of great good humor, or both, you do not regret its absence."[1] His nephew, Sir George Otto Trevelyan, adds that his head was massive and his features of a powerful and rugged cast. Despite his carelessness in dress Macaulay was a lion in society on account both of his good nature and of his great power. A remark has been attributed to Gladstone to the effect that few men had ever attained such wide and honorable renown and such immense distinction before middle life.

His good nature may have many other names all equally applicable. He was noble—with the help of his brother Henry he paid off all of his father's debts, he supported his brothers and sisters; he was benevolent—he assisted those in trouble, whether known to him or not and sometimes whether solicited or not; he was generous—his nephews and nieces were always receiving treats; he was magnanimous—he offered his resignation to the government rather than oppose his father's wishes concerning a proposed parliamentary measure, he relinquished

---

[1] From Praed's Introduction to Knight's *Quarterly Magazine*, quoted by Trevelyan, vol. I, p. 117.

his parliamentary career to go to India in order to secure a competence for his family; he was sincere—he voted for a bill which abolished his own office and left him in hard financial straits; he was loyal—giving to party and to friends both time and labor needed for other and greater things; he had sweetness—in trouble he showed sunniest radiance, in gladness he was the life of the home, playing, capping verses, making puns, composing verses, which he always attributed to the "Judicious Poet"; he loved all children—witness the excursions, the treats, the valentines; he had such sensibility that he was easily touched to tears by pathos in life or in books; he was altogether such a man as we love. Even his severest critics yield hearty admiration to him as a man. One says: ". . . as a son, as a brother, and an uncle—it is only the barest justice to say that he appears to have touched the furthest verge of human virtue, sweetness, and generosity." [1]

Macaulay's power had many phases. He was an enormous reader, he had a phenomenal memory and a remarkable capacity for work. He was an orator and a conversationalist, an essayist and an historian, a statesman and a man of practical affairs, a student and a poet. Able to take in a page at a glance, reading was play; not needing to commit anything to memory, for everything seemed to stick forever, he was able to repeat whole books; vigorous, he could write on an essay before breakfast, perform his official business during the day, attend a public function in the early evening, and spend the rest of it and half the night in the House of Commons. When he rose to speak in Parliament it came to be a summons for the members to fill the benches and in social life his powers of conversation can be compared with those of Dr. Johnson only. Brilliant, witty, and fertile in mind, he was a "combination of public spirit, political instinct, and legitimate self-assertion": [2] prudent, energetic, and self-reliant, he was a "combination of literary power, his-

[1] *Thomas B. Macaulay*, by J. Cotter Morison, p. 18.
[2] Trevelyan, vol. I, p. 180.

torical learning, and practical familiarity with the conduct of great affairs."[1]

Many critics have tried to patronize Macaulay, particularly those of the generation following his. But this attempt is due to the absolute change in the attitude toward life of their day and of his. He belonged to that optimistic band of actors whose work culminated about 1830; they belonged to the reactionary band of analysts, for if one period produces, the next criticizes, if one period praises, the next blames.

III. WRITINGS

Macaulay's writings fall into three divisions, essays, history, and poetry. The essays in turn, forty in number, are most easily subdivided into the following groups: English history, foreign history, controversy, criticism, and biography. Of the first group those on Lord Clive and on Warren Hastings are the most famous, of the second that on Von Ranke is the most celebrated, of the third those on Mill had the most weight, of the fourth that on Addison is the widest known, and of the fifth that on Johnson is a classic.

All of the essays were and are very popular. They gave their author an unprecedented fame and added vastly to the influence and to the circulation of *The Edinburgh Review*, in which all but the biographical group appeared. They introduced many to the study of the subjects of which they treated, they aroused thought, and they always inculcated honest, strong, manly belief. Further, Macaulay did much for the essay as a form of literary composition. His predecessors, such as Bacon, Steele, and Addison, were crude; his contemporaries, such as Lamb and Hazlitt, developed to a high degree the chatty species, others pushed forward the critical variety; Macaulay in his practice made the general form more definite, and polished the historical variety nearly to perfection.

[1] Ibid., vol. II, p. 374.

There has been much discussion about Macaulay's *History*, the full title of which is *The History of England from the Accession of James II*. It had such an immense success that most writers seem called upon to pull it down from its high place. The author said in 1841, "I shall not be satisfied unless I produce something which shall for a few days supersede the last fashionable novel on the tables of young ladies." He succeeded. Edition after edition was called for. The sale was so large that his publishers in 1856 sent him as only one of many payments a check for nearly $100,000. The book was translated into many languages. It was praised by the greatest men of the world and a group of workingmen passed him a vote of thanks for writing a history that they could understand.

The reason why critics from about 1856 to a recent date have been so ready to throw stones at this shining mark is, apart from the fact of his eminence, because the conception of history has changed. Macaulay wrote, from the political and social standpoint, history that is literature, being among the first to introduce the social element. Later, history was woven from society, politics, and business. Now to these three another and a dominant strand is being added—the working of the human mind. But the sneers are fading away. Just as the value of Herodotus and of Thucydides is recognized though they did not write in accordance with the twentieth century plan, so Macaulay is coming back to his own.

The secret and the effect of the *History* have been thus most admirably expressed by William Roscoe Thayer: "He entertains you with a panoramic wealth of details, but never allows you to grope for the plot. When you close his book and ponder over it, it is as if you had been watching a Roman legion on the march. The sun flashes from the helmets and shields and spears of the cohorts as they wind like a huge and gem-scaled serpent over the plain. Now they are hidden by a wood; now they emerge into the open, and the sunbeams gild their sinuous line, which throbs as if every stride were a pulse. Here they glide into a walled town and are lost except for a casual sparkle or the beat of a distant drum; but anon they flash again into view and begin to curve along the mountain side or to coil around a fortressed crag. And so on and on, the embodiment of disciplined, tireless force, of agile, elastic force, with rhythmic sweep and gleaming form and with an indefectible purpose." [1]

Macaulay wrote poetry all of his life, his first recorded efforts belonging probably to his eighth year. His facility in composition was phenomenal. For hours at a time he could produce in play, for the amusement of the home circle, a continuous flow of verses, all ascribed to "The Judicious Poet." In college his poetic power twice won him the Chancellor's medal. During his voyages to and from India and while there he read and reread enormous quantities of Latin and of Greek. With his mind filled with ancient life, his ever-ready poetic ability used this abundant material and about 1838 we have mention of his putting some of the legends of Rome into ballad form. Ballads always intensely interested him and he felt that he should like to restore to poetry that of which it had been robbed by history. For he believed that the stories to be found in the early books of the Latin historian, Livy, were taken from the lost ballads of the early Romans. This belief was shared by Niebuhr, the German scholar, and by Dr. Arnold, the great Headmaster of Rugby, who saw two of the ballads and, as Macaulay says in a letter to Napier, the editor of *The Edinburgh Review*, "wrote to me in such terms of eulogy that I have been induced to correct and complete them. There are four of them, and I think that, though they are but trifles, they may pass for scholarlike and not inelegant trifles." [2]

The poems, often composed during his walks, took form slowly, being polished and changed many times, occasionally for the sake of topographical accuracy. Some of these changes were suggested during his tour of Italy in 1838 when he got

---
[1] *North American Review*, December, 1909.
[2] Trevelyan, vol. II, p. 103.

many touches of local color for future use, his diary at this time being full of observations of Italian scenery and locality. Often there are direct entries concerning the ballads; thus on November 9, 1838, he says, "I meditated some verses for my ballad of 'Romulus,' but only made one stanza to my satisfaction." This poem was later published as "The Prophecy of Capys." As they were perfected we hear of their being submitted to Ellis, a tried friend of long standing and likewise an ex-Fellow of Trinity, who was heartily interested and suggested a few changes here and there.

The volume, *The Lays of Ancient Rome*, appeared in 1842. Previous to its publication, Macaulay stipulated to Longman, his publisher, that there should be no puffing, and asked it of Napier as a personal favor that his name and his writings should never be mentioned in *The Review*. As soon as the book was given to the public it "sold like Scott's most popular poetry" as Leslie Stephen says.[1] And even such an old adversary as Professor Wilson "greeted it in *Blackwood's Magazine* with a pæan of hearty, unqualified panegyric."[2] The popularity has continued. The vigorous swing of the strong manly thoughts appeal to the public as much as ever. Readers have approved the Lays and now they are included among the classics of English Literature.

Previous to the publication of the Lays, Macaulay had produced three other poems well qualified to stand side by side with his later songs. These are "Ivry, A Song of the Huguenots" (1824), "The Battle of Naseby" (1824), and "The Armada" (1832). These are trumpet-notes of triumph, Hebraic songs of victory whose theme is the overthrow of the mighty oppressor: mediæval religious intolerance of the French is avenged, English political pride is dethroned, and Spanish arrogance humiliated.

[1] *Hours in a Library*, vol. III, p. 231.
[2] Trevelyan, vol. II, p. 110.

IV. STYLE

When Jeffrey acknowledged the receipt of Macaulay's manuscript of the *Essay on Milton* he wrote, "The more I think, the less I can conceive where you picked up that style."[1] And Frederic Harrison speaks of a passage in that essay as "vigorous invective in the style of Cicero."[2] Is not this a hint as to the secret of that wonderful style? "Soak your mind in Cicero" was Macaulay's advice and practice when in college. Further he read and reread Cicero all his life. So it is natural that his style should be Ciceronian. Furthermore Cicero was an orator, so it is only to be expected that Macaulay's style should be oratorical. And that is what it is. We unconsciously imagine the author as delivering his composition to an audience. The Latin style, again, constantly uses antithesis, one part of an idea being set over against another. There is also much ornamentation. Both of these characteristics are abundant in Macaulay. But he has the knack of breaking from long sentences into short ones for the sake of emphasis and in a climax.

His style is above all things clear. That no one can fail to grasp his meaning is a fact upon which he prided himself. Narrative power he has, too, being one of the best story-tellers. And he can interest and hold the attention of his readers, a characteristic due largely to his ability to use brilliant illustration, his mind being so well stored that scores of precedents and examples were always ready with which to make clear or to sustain. His portraits of persons are unique: his knowledge immense. Into one sentence he crams the result of vast reading. Like all the Scotch he can reduce men to classes and events to principles. Through it all he is intensely patriotic.

Macaulay's writings are in many respects models. He greatly influenced all later writers. For the paragraph he did much. In his essays we have definite topic sentences definitely

---

[1] Trevelyan, vol. I, p. 117.
[2] *Studies in Early Victorian Literature*, p. 79.

developed by regular methods since formulated in the textbooks of rhetoric. He knew the art of transition. And the whole gives a well-ordered panoramic view or expository conception. In other words, he thought clearly, knew just what he wanted to say, and how to say it. To-day the makers of textbooks quote from him copiously, in grammar for his precision, in rhetoric for his felicitous choice of words and for his power to express his exact shade of meaning as well as for the arrangement and presentation of his thought. His success is doubtless due to his infinite capacity for revision, in which Stevenson resembles him.

Unfortunately for themselves some of his critics have derided what they call his "rhetoric." But what is the purpose of rhetoric, that is technique in writing, if not to produce desired effects? That sneer, however, is nearly forgotten and credit is now being given his verbal artistry because it is the work of an artist.

V. PLACE AND SERVICE

During his life Macaulay had success in abundance, political, literary, and social. It began in early youth and continued in growing measure till his death. It is so great as to excite wonder. At twenty-five he had achieved fame in literature, at thirty he had become a Member of Parliament, at thirty-four he had been made one of the rulers of India, at thirty-nine he had reached the position of a Cabinet Minister, at forty-three he was read over the educated world, at forty-eight he had reached eminence as an historian, at fifty-seven he had been raised to the Peerage, at fifty-nine he died, rich, powerful, honored, all through his own abilities alone. But immediately there set in a reaction. The critics, and he had many because he had a multitude of readers and no one can please everyone, said he was shallow, glittering, a mere artist in words without philosophy and without insight. They picked such minute errors in his *History* that "These allegations savor a little c the technical knowledge of an advocate at the criminal bar retained for the defense."[1] It became fashionable to deride Macaulay, the trick being caught by those who had not read him. So it continued for fifty years. But now there is a change. The third generation is considering him without bias and without personal interest. And what is the result? The critics are writing articles with such titles as "The Revival of Macaulay," "The Vitality of Macaulay," "The Enduring Characteristics of Macaulay."

Therefore because he knew how to write brilliantly, how to interest, how to arouse thought, how to stir the heart, how to hold up to admiration "whatsoever things are true, whatsoever things are honest, whatsoever things are just, whatsoever things are pure, whatsoever things are lovely, whatsoever things are of good report" and how to condemn unsparingly and indignantly the reverse, let us accept him thankfully as the most enduring and the most typical English writer of the early portion of the Nineteenth Century, "a very great man of letters and an almost unsurpassed leader to reading."[2]

VI. CHRONOLOGICAL TABLE

1800, October 25, born at Rothley Temple, Leicestershire.
1812, Mr. Preston's School at Little Shelford.
1818, Trinity College, Cambridge.
1819, First Chancellor's Medal.
1821, Craven Scholarship. Second Chancellor's Medal.
1822, B. A.
1824, Fellow of Trinity.
1825, Article on Milton in August *Edinburgh Review*.
1826, Called to the Bar.
1828, Commissioner of Bankruptcy.
1830, M. P. for borough of Calne.
1832, Commissioner of Board of Control. Later Secretary.
1833, M. P. for Leeds.

[1] Henry D. Sedgwick, Jr., in *The Atlantic Monthly*, August, 1899.
[2] George Saintsbury, *Corrected Impressions* (1895), p. 97.

1834, Legal Adviser to the Supreme Council of India.
1838, Return to England.
1839, M. P. for Edinburgh.   Secretary at War.
1841, Reëlected from Edinburgh.
1842, *Lays of Ancient Rome.*
1843, Collected Edition of Essays.
1846, Paymaster-general.
1847, Defeated at Edinburgh.
1848, *History of England from the Accession of James II*, vols. I, II.
1852, Reëlected from Edinburgh.   Serious illness.
1857, Elevated to the Peerage.
1859, December 28, died at Holly Lodge, Kensington.

VII. LIST OF MACAULAY'S ESSAYS

1. *English History Group:*
    Milton, August, 1825.
    Hallam's *Constitutional History*, September, 1828.
    Lord Nugent's *Memorials of Hampden*, December, 1831.
    Burleigh and His Times, April, 1832.
    Horace Walpole, October, 1833.
    William Pitt, Earl of Chatham, January, 1834.
    Sir James Mackintosh, July, 1835.
    Sir William Temple, October, 1838.
    Lord Clive, January, 1840.
    Warren Hastings, October, 1841.
    The Earl of Chatham, October, 1844.
2. *Foreign History Group:*
    Machiavelli, March, 1827.
    Mirabeau, July, 1832.
    Lord Mahon's *War of the Succession in Spain*, January, 1833.
    Von Ranke's *History of the Popes*, October, 1840.
    Frederick the Great, April, 1842.
    Barère's *Memoirs*, April, 1844.
3. *Controversial Group:*
    Mill's *Essay on Government*, March, June, and October, 1829.
    Southey's *Colloquies on Society*, January, 1830.

Sadler's *Law of Population*, July, 1830, January, 1831.
Gladstone on Church and State, April, 1839.
4. *Critical Group:*
John Dryden, January, 1828.
History, May, 1828.
Mr. Robert Montgomery's *Poems*, April, 1830.
Southey's Edition of *The Pilgrim's Progress*, December, 1830.
Moore's *Life of Lord Byron*, June, 1831.
Croker's Edition of Boswell's *Life of Johnson*, September, 1831.
Lord Bacon, July, 1837.
Leigh Hunt's *Comic Dramatists of the Restoration*, 1841.
Diary and *Letters* of Madame D'Arblay, January, 1843.
The Life and Writings of Addison, July, 1843.
5. *Biographical Group:*
Francis Atterbury, December, 1853.
John Bunyan, May, 1854.
Oliver Goldsmith, February, 1856.
Samuel Johnson, December, 1856.
William Pitt, January, 1859.

VIII. REFERENCES

Biography
Macaulay's *Life and Letters*, by Sir G. O. Trevelyan (1876).
Criticism
Macaulay, by Sir Richard C. Jebb, M. P. (1900).
Articles by
Henry D. Sedgwick, Jr., in *The Atlantic Monthly*, August, 1899.
Prof. A. V. Dicey of Oxford in *The Nation*, May 15, 1902.
W. R. Thayer in *The North American Review*, December, 1909.

IX. OUTLINE OF MACAULAY'S PREFACE TO THE LAYS

A. What is called the history of the kings and early consuls of Rome is fabulous, for
  i. The public records were destroyed by the Gauls.
  ii. The oldest annals were compiled more than a century and a half later.

INTRODUCTION

   iii. The writers of the Augustan Age admit the inaccuracy of their material.
B. The early history of Rome is far more poetical than anything else in Latin Literature, for
   i. The poetical character of the events is discernible in all the histories.
   ii. In the days of Plutarch there were skeptics concerning its truth.
C. Perizonius put forward a theory, revived by Niebuhr, and adopted by such scholars as Dr. Arnold, that there was an early Latin Literature, now lost, consisting of ballads.
   i. This is probable, for
      a. All human beings long for information of the past,
      b. Only enlightened communities have access to books,
      c. All races have such a ballad literature, as is shown by
         1. The Germans,
         2. The Gauls,
         3. The English, and others.
   ii. There is direct evidence for it, for it is referred to by
      a. Ennius,
      b. Fabius,
      c. Cato, the Censor,
      d. Valerius Maximus,
      e. Varro.
D. That this early poetry perished is not strange, for
   i. The Greek genius completely triumphed over the public mind of Italy.
E. The process by which the old songs were transmuted into the form which they now wear is: ballads became funeral panegyrics, which became chronicles, which in turn became part of the present histories. This is proved by
   i. The stories of Edgar in Hume's *History*, in English.
   ii. The story of the heirs of Carrion in Mariana's *History*, in Spanish.
F. To reverse that process, to transform some portions of early Roman history back into the poetry out of which they were made, is the object of this work [the Lays].
G. In the following poems the author speaks, not in his own person,

but in the persons of ancient minstrels who know only what a Roman citizen, born three or four hundred years before the Christian era, may be supposed to have known and who feel as such would feel.

X. Legends Underlying the Lays and Macaulay's Introduction to "Horatius"

To understand the poems it is necessary to know the conditions. In ancient times Italy was split up into many sections, such as Etruria and Latium, in which dwelt rather distinct tribes, whose cities were joined into loosely formed confederacies. The cities were ruled in paternal fashion by a chief man. In the course of time Rome became much larger than the other cities and the ruler was given the title of king. Several of the kings belonged to one family, the Tarquins. They were bad men and bad kings. Finally they were banished and the kingship abolished because Sextus, one of the sons of Tarquinius Superbus (the haughty) outraged Lucretia, the virtuous wife of his cousin, Tarquinius Collatinus.

But Tarquinius Superbus, not content to be banished, made four attempts to regain the throne. The first attempt was made through his friends in the city but was frustrated. The second was made by the aid of the people of Tarquinii and of Veii, who were repulsed in battle. The third attempt was made with the support of Lars Porsena of Clusium who ruled all of Etruria. How the attacking party failed to capture the city is told in "Horatius." The fourth was made with the help of his son-in-law, Octavius Mamilius of Tusculum. Its failure is told in "The Battle of the Lake Regillus."

Macaulay's introduction to "Horatius" makes the following points:

1. The story of Horatius Cocles had a poetical origin.
2. There are several versions, differing in minor points, whose discrepancies are easily explained, as is seen in English Literature, on the supposition that there were two ballads

on the defense of the bridge, one preferred by the multitude, the other by the Horatian house.
3. "The ballad is supposed to have been made about a hundred and twenty years after the war which it celebrates, and just before the taking of Rome by the Gauls. The author seems to have been an honest citizen, proud of the military glory of his country, sick of the disputes of factions and much given to pining after good old times which had never really existed. The allusion, however, to the partial manner in which the public lands were allotted could proceed only from a plebeian; and the allusion to the fraudulent sale of spoils marks the date of the poem, and shows that the poet shared in the general discontent with which the proceedings of Camillus, after the taking of Veii, were regarded."
4. The penultimate syllable of Porsena is short on the authority of Martial, Horace, and Silius Italicus, Niebuhr notwithstanding.
5. "Niebuhr's supposition that each of the three defenders of the bridge was the representative of one of the three patrician tribes is both ingenious and probable, and has been adopted."

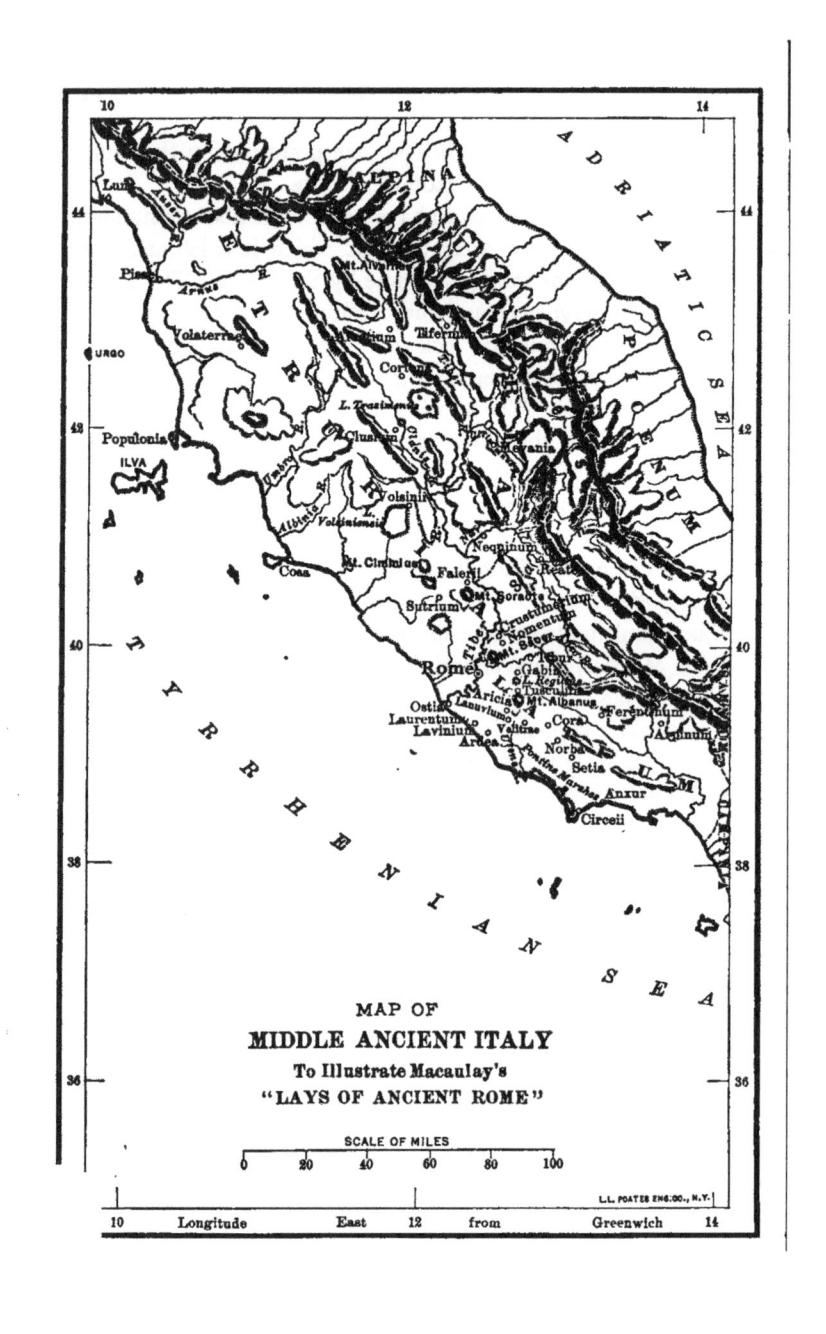

MAP OF
MIDDLE ANCIENT ITALY
To Illustrate Macaulay's
"LAYS OF ANCIENT ROME"

LAYS OF ANCIENT ROME

HORATIUS

A LAY MADE ABOUT THE YEAR OF THE CITY CCCLX

I

Lars Porsena of Clusium
  By the Nine Gods he swore
That the great house of Tarquin
  Should suffer wrong no more.
By the Nine Gods he swore it,
  And named a trysting day,[1]
And bade his messengers ride forth,
East and west and south and north,
  To summon his array.

II

East and west and south and north
  The messengers ride fast,
And tower and town and cottage
  Have heard the trumpet's blast.
Shame on the false Etruscan
  Who lingers in his home,
When Porsena of Clusium
  Is on the march for Rome!

III

The horsemen and the footmen
  Are pouring in amain [2]
From many a stately market-place,
  From many a fruitful plain;

[1] Meeting day.   [2] In force.

From many a lonely hamlet,
　　Which, hid by beech and pine,
Like an eagle's nest, hangs on the crest
　　Of purple Apennine;

IV

From lordly Volaterræ,
　　Where scowls the far-famed hold [1]
Piled by the hands of giants
　　For godlike kings of old;
From seagirt Populonia,
　　Whose sentinels descry
Sardinia's snowy mountain-tops
　　Fringing the southern sky;

V

From the proud mart [2] of Pisæ,
　　Queen of the western waves,
Where ride Massilia's triremes
　　Heavy with fair-haired slaves;
From where sweet Clanis wanders
　　Through corn and vines and flowers;
From where Cortona lifts to heaven
　　Her diadem of towers.

VI

Tall are the oaks whose acorns
　　Drop in dark Auser's rill;
Fat are the stags that champ [3] the boughs
　　Of the Ciminian hill;
Beyond all streams Clitumnus
　　Is to the herdsman dear;
Best of all pools the fowler loves
　　The great Volsinian mere.

[1] Stronghold, fort.　　[2] Market.　　[3] Bite repeatedly and impatiently.

VII

But now no stroke of woodman
  Is heard by Auser's rill;
No hunter tracks the stag's green path
  Up the Ciminian hill;
Unwatched along Clitumnus
  Grazes the milk-white steer;
Unharmed the waterfowl may dip
  In the Volsinian mere.

VIII

The harvests of Arretium,
  This year, old men shall reap;
This year, young boys in Umbro
  Shall plunge the struggling sheep;
And in the vats of Luna,
  This year, the must [1] shall foam
Round the white feet of laughing girls
  Whose sires have marched to Rome.

IX

There be thirty chosen prophets,
  The wisest of the land,
Who alway by Lars Porsena
  Both morn and evening stand;
Evening and morn the Thirty
  Have turned the verses o'er,
Traced from the right on linen white
  By mighty seers [2] of yore. [3]

X

And with one voice [4] the Thirty
  Have their glad answer given:
"Go forth, go forth, Lars Porsena;
  Go forth, beloved of Heaven;

---

[1] Juice from the grape.
[2] One who foresees the future.
[3] Old.
[4] All agreed.

Go, and return in glory
  To Clusium's royal dome,
And hang round Nurscia's altars
  The golden shields of Rome."

XI

And now hath every city
  Sent up her tale [1] of men;
The foot are fourscore thousand,
  The horse are thousands ten:
Before the gates of Sutrium
  Is met the great array.
A proud man was Lars Porsena
  Upon the trysting day.

XII

For all the Etruscan armies
  Were ranged beneath his eye,
And many a banished Roman,
  And many a stout ally;
And with a mighty following
  To join the muster came
The Tusculan Mamilius,
  Prince of the Latian name.

XIII

But by the yellow Tiber
  Was tumult and affright:
From all the spacious champaign
  To Rome men took their flight.
A mile around the city
  The throng stopped up the ways;
A fearful sight it was to see
  Through two long nights and days.

---

[1] Counted share.

XIV

For aged folks on crutches,
  And women great with child,
And mothers sobbing over babes
  That clung to them and smiled,
And sick men borne in litters [1]
  High on the necks of slaves,
And troops of sunburnt husbandmen
  With reaping-hooks and staves,

XV

And droves of mules and asses
  Laden with skins of wine,
And endless flocks of goats and sheep,
  And endless herds of kine,[2]
And endless trains of wagons
  That creaked beneath the weight
Of corn-sacks and of household goods,
  Choked every roaring gate.

XVI

Now, from the rock Tarpeian,
  Could the wan burghers [3] spy
The line of blazing villages
  Red in the midnight sky.
The Fathers of the City,
  They sat [4] all night and day,
For every hour some horseman came
  With tidings of dismay.

XVII

To eastward and to westward
  Have spread the Tuscan bands;
Nor house, nor fence, nor dovecote [5]
  In Crustumerium stands.

---

[1] A couch on shafts borne by men.   [3] Citizens.   [5] House for doves.
[2] Old plural of cow.   [4] Continued in meeting.

Verbenna down to Ostia
  Hath wasted all the plain;
Astur hath stormed Janiculum,
  And the stout guards are slain.

XVIII

I wis, in all the Senate,
  There was no heart so bold,
But sore it ached, and fast it beat,
  When that ill news was told.
Forthwith up rose the Consul,[1]
  Up rose the Fathers all;
In haste they girded up their gowns,
  And hied [2] them to the wall.

XIX

They held a council standing
  Before the River-Gate;
Short time was there, ye well may guess,
  For musing [3] or debate.
Out spake the Consul roundly:
  "The bridge must straight go down;
For, since Janiculum is lost,
  Naught else can save the town."

XX

Just then a scout came flying,
  All wild with haste and fear:
"To arms! to arms! Sir Consul;
  Lars Porsena is here."
On the low hills to westward
  The Consul fixed his eye,
And saw the swarthy storm of dust
  Rise fast along the sky.

---

[1] Chief official of Rome.   [2] Hastened.   [3] Slow thinking.

XXI

And nearer fast and nearer
  Doth the red whirlwind come;
And louder still and still more loud,
From underneath that rolling cloud,
Is heard the trumpet's war-note proud,
  The trampling, and the hum.
And plainly and more plainly
  Now through the gloom appears,
Far to left and far to right,
In broken gleams of dark-blue light,
The long array of helmets bright,
  The long array of spears.

XXII

And plainly and more plainly,
  Above that glimmering line,
Now might ye see the banners
  Of twelve fair cities shine;
But the banner of proud Clusium
  Was highest of them all,
The terror of the Umbrian,
  The terror of the Gaul.

XXIII

And plainly and more plainly
  Now might the burghers know,
By port [1] and vest,[2] by horse and crest,[3]
  Each warlike Lucumo.
There Cilnius of Arretium
  On his fleet roan [4] was seen;
And Astur of the fourfold shield,
Girt with the brand [5] none else may wield,

---

[1] Bearing.
[2] Dress.
[3] Ornament on top of the helmet.
[4] Chestnut-colored horse.
[5] Sword.

Tolumnius with the belt of gold,
And dark Verbenna from the hold
　By reedy Thrasymene.

XXIV

Fast by the royal standard,
　O'erlooking all the war,
Lars Porsena of Clusium
　Sat in his ivory car.[1]
By the right wheel rode Mamilius
　Prince of the Latian name;
And by the left false Sextus,
　That wrought the deed of shame.

XXV

But when the face of Sextus
　Was seen among the foes,
A yell that rent the firmament
　From all the town arose.
On the housetops was no woman
　But spat towards him and hissed,
No child but screamed out curses,
　And shook its little fist.

XXVI

But the Consul's brow was sad,
　And the Consul's speech was low,
And darkly looked he at the wall,
　And darkly at the foe.
"Their van will be upon us
　Before the bridge goes down;
And if they once may win the bridge,
　What hope to save the town?"

---

[1] Chariot.

XXVII

Then out spake brave Horatius,
  The Captain of the Gate:
"To every man upon this earth
  Death cometh soon or late.
And how can man die better
  Than facing fearful odds,
For the ashes of his fathers,
  And the temples of his Gods,

XXVIII

"And for the tender mother
  Who dandled him to rest,
And for the wife who nurses
  His baby at her breast,
And for the holy maidens
  Who feed the eternal flame,
To save them from false Sextus
  That wrought the deed of shame?

XXIX

"Hew [1] down the bridge, Sir Consul,
  With all the speed ye may;
I, with two more to help me,
  Will hold the foe in play.
In yon strait path a thousand
  May well be stopped by three.
Now who will stand on either hand,
  And keep the bridge with me?"

XXX

Then out spake Spurius Lartius;
  A Ramnian proud was he:
"Lo, I will stand at thy right hand,
  And keep the bridge with thee."

[1] Cut.

And out spake strong Herminius; 245
  Of Titian blood was he:
"I will abide on thy left side,
  And keep the bridge with thee."

XXXI

"Horatius," quoth the Consul,
  "As thou sayest, so let it be." 250
And straight against that great array
  Forth went the dauntless Three.
For Romans in Rome's quarrel
  Spared neither land nor gold,
Nor son nor wife, nor limb nor life, 255
  In the brave days of old.

XXXII

Then none was for a party;[1]
  Then all were for the state;
Then the great man helped the poor,
  And the poor man loved the great; 260
Then lands were fairly portioned;
  Then spoils[2] were fairly sold:
The Romans were like brothers
  In the brave days of old.

XXXIII

Now Roman is to Roman 265
  More hateful than a foe,
And the Tribunes beard[3] the high,
  And the Fathers grind[4] the low.
As we wax[5] hot in faction,
  In battle we wax cold; 270
Wherefore men fight not as they fought
  In the brave days of old.

---

[1] Political group or faction.
[2] Things captured in war.
[3] Oppose to the face.
[4] Oppress.
[5] Grow.

XXXIV

Now while the Three were tightening
   Their harness [1] on their backs,
The Consul was the foremost man
   To take in hand an ax;
And Fathers mixed with Commons,
   Seized hatchet, bar, and crow,
And smote upon the planks above,
   And loosed the props below.

XXXV

Meanwhile the Tuscan army,
   Right glorious to behold,
Came flashing back the noonday light,
Rank behind rank, like surges bright
   Of a broad sea of gold.
Four hundred trumpets sounded
   A peal of warlike glee,
As that great host, with measured tread,
And spears advanced, and ensigns [2] spread,
Rolled slowly toward the bridge's head,
   Where stood the dauntless Three.

XXXVI

The Three stood calm and silent,
   And looked upon the foes,
And a great shout of laughter
   From all the vanguard rose;
And forth three chiefs came spurring
   Before that deep array;
To earth they sprang, their swords they drew,
And lifted high their shields, and flew
   To win the narrow way;

---

[1] Armor.   [2] Standards, insignia.

XXXVII

Aunus from green Tifernum
  Lord of the Hill of Vines;
And Seius, whose eight hundred slaves
  Sicken in Ilva's mines;
And Picus, long to Clusium
  Vassal [1] in peace and war,
Who led to fight his Umbrian powers [2]
From that gray crag where, girt with towers,
The fortress of Nequinum lowers
  O'er the pale waves of Nar.

XXXVIII

Stout Lartius hurled down Aunus
  Into the stream beneath;
Herminius struck at Seius,
  And clove [3] him to the teeth;
At Picus brave Horatius
  Darted one fiery thrust,
And the proud Umbrian's gilded arms
  Clashed in the bloody dust.

XXXIX

Then Ocnus of Falerii
  Rushed on the Roman Three;
And Lausulus of Urgo,
  The rover [4] of the sea;
And Aruns of Volsinium,
  Who slew the great wild boar,
The great wild boar that had his den
Amidst the reeds of Cosa's fen,
And wasted fields, and slaughtered men,
  Along Albinia's shore.

---

[1] Dependent.
[2] Forces of soldiers.
[3] Split.
[4] Pirate.

XL

Herminius smote down Aruns;
    Lartius laid Ocnus low;
Right to the heart of Lausulus
    Horatius sent a blow.
"Lie there," he cried, "fell [1] pirate!
    No more, aghast and pale,
From Ostia's walls the crowd shall mark
The track of thy destroying bark.[2]
No more Campania's hinds [3] shall fly
To woods and caverns when they spy
    Thy thrice accursed sail."

XLI

But now no sound of laughter
    Was heard among the foes;
A wild and wrathful clamor
    From all the vanguard rose.
Six spears' length from the entrance
    Halted that deep array,
And for a space no man came forth
    To win the narrow way.

XLII

But hark! the cry is Astur:
    And lo! the ranks divide;
And the great Lord of Luna
    Comes with his stately stride.
Upon his ample shoulders
    Clangs loud the fourfold shield,
And in his hand he shakes the brand
    Which none but he can wield.

---

[1] Fierce, ruthless.   [2] Ship.   [3] Peasants.

XLIII

He smiled on those bold Romans
  A smile serene and high;
He eyed the flinching Tuscans,
  And scorn was in his eye.
Quoth he, "The she-wolf's litter
  Stand savagely at bay;
But will ye dare to follow,
  If Astur clears the way?"

XLIV

Then, whirling up his broadsword
  With both hands to the height,
He rushed against Horatius,
  And smote with all his might.
With shield and blade [1] Horatius
  Right deftly turned the blow.
The blow, though turned, came yet too nigh;
It missed his helm,[2] but gashed his thigh:
The Tuscans raised a joyful cry
  To see the red blood flow.

XLV

He reeled, and on Herminius
  He leaned one breathing-space;
Then, like a wild cat mad with wounds,
  Sprang right at Astur's face;
Through teeth and skull and helmet
  So fierce a thrust he sped,
The good sword stood a handbreadth out
  Behind the Tuscan's head.

XLVI

And the great Lord of Luna
  Fell at that deadly stroke,

---

[1] Sword.   [2] Helmet.

As falls on Mount Alvernus
  A thunder-smitten oak.
Far o'er the crashing forest
  The giant arms lie spread;
And the pale augurs, muttering low,
  Gaze on the blasted head.

XLVII

On Astur's throat Horatius
  Right firmly pressed his heel,
And thrice and four times tugged amain,
  Ere he wrenched out the steel.
"And see," he cried, "the welcome,
  Fair guests, that waits you here!
What noble Lucumo comes next
  To taste our Roman cheer?"

XLVIII

But at his haughty challenge
  A sullen murmur ran,
Mingled of wrath and shame and dread,
  Along that glittering van.
There lacked not men of prowess,[1]
  Nor men of lordly race;
For all Etruria's noblest
  Were round the fatal place.

XLIX

But all Etruria's noblest
  Felt their hearts sink to see
On the earth the bloody corpses,
  In the path the dauntless Three;
And from the ghastly entrance
  Where those bold Romans stood,

[1] Bravery.

All shrank, like boys who unaware,
Ranging the woods to start a hare,
Come to the mouth of the dark lair [1]
Where, growling low, a fierce old bear
  Lies amidst bones and blood.

L

Was none who would be foremost
  To lead such dire attack;
But those behind cried "Forward!"
  And those before cried "Back!"
And backward now and forward
  Wavers the deep array;
And on the tossing sea of steel
To and fro the standards reel,
And the victorious trumpet-peal
  Dies fitfully away.

LI

Yet one man for one moment
  Stood out before the crowd;
Well known was he to all the Three,
  And they gave him greeting loud:
"Now welcome, welcome, Sextus!
  Now welcome to thy home!
Why dost thou stay, and turn away?
  Here lies the road to Rome."

LII

Thrice looked he at the city,
  Thrice looked he at the dead;
And thrice came on in fury,
  And thrice turned back in dread;

---

[1] Den.

And, white with fear and hatred,
  Scowled at the narrow way,
Where, wallowing in a pool of blood,
  The bravest Tuscans lay.

LIII

But meanwhile ax and lever
  Have manfully been plied;
And now the bridge hangs tottering
  Above the boiling tide.
"Come back, come back, Horatius!"
  Loud cried the Fathers all.
"Back, Lartius! back, Herminius!
  Back, ere the ruin fall!"

LIV

Back darted Spurius Lartius,
  Herminius darted back;
And, as they passed, beneath their feet
  They felt the timbers crack.
But when they turned their faces,
  And on the farther shore
Saw brave Horatius stand alone,
  They would have crossed once more.

LV

But with a crash like thunder
  Fell every loosened beam,
And, like a dam, the mighty wreck
  Lay right athwart[1] the stream.
And a long shout of triumph
  Rose from the walls of Rome,
As to the highest turret-tops
  Was splashed the yellow foam.

[1] Across.

LVI

And, like a horse unbroken
   When first he feels the rein,
The furious river struggled hard,
   And tossed his tawny mane,
And burst the curb, and bounded
   Rejoicing to be free,
And whirling down, in fierce career,
Battlement and plank and pier,[1]
   Rushed headlong to the sea.

LVII

Alone stood brave Horatius,
   But constant[2] still in mind,
Thrice thirty thousand foes before
   And the broad flood behind.
"Down with him!" cried false Sextus,
   With a smile on his pale face.
"Now yield thee," cried Lars Porsena,
   "Now yield thee to our grace."[3]

LVIII

Round turned he, as not deigning[4]
   Those craven[5] ranks to see;
Naught spake he to Lars Porsena,
   To Sextus naught spake he;
But he saw on Palatinus
   The white porch of his home,
And he spake to the noble river
   That rolls by the towers of Rome:

LIX

"Oh, Tiber, father Tiber!
   To whom the Romans pray,

---

[1] Support.   [2] Unshaken.   [3] Mercy.   [4] Condescending.   [5] Cowardly.

HORATIUS

A Roman's life, a Roman's arms,
  Take thou in charge this day!"
So he spake, and speaking sheathed
  The good sword by his side,
And with his harness on his back,
  Plunged headlong in the tide.

LX

No sound of joy or sorrow
  Was heard from either bank,
But friends and foes in dumb surprise,
With parted lips and straining eyes,
  Stood gazing where he sank;
And when above the surges [1]
  They saw his crest appear,
All Rome sent forth a rapturous cry,
And even the ranks of Tuscany
  Could scarce forbear to cheer.

LXI

But fiercely ran the current,
  Swollen high by months of rain;
And fast his blood was flowing,
  And he was sore in pain,
And heavy with his armor,
  And spent [2] with changing blows;
And oft they thought him sinking,
  But still again he rose.

LXII

Never, I ween, did swimmer,
  In such an evil case,[3]
Struggle through such a raging flood
  Safe to the landing place;

---

[1] Waves.   [2] Exhausted.   [3] Condition.

But his limbs were borne up bravely
  By the brave heart within,
And our good father Tiber
  Bore bravely up his chin.

LXIII

"Curse on him!" quoth false Sextus;
  "Will not the villain drown?
But for this stay,[1] ere close of day
  We should have sacked the town!"
"Heaven help him!" quoth Lars Porsena,
  "And bring him safe to shore;
For such a gallant feat[2] of arms
  Was never seen before."

LXIV

And now he feels the bottom;
  Now on dry earth he stands;
Now round him throng the Fathers
  To press his gory hands;
And now, with shouts and clapping,
  And noise of weeping loud,
He enters through the River-Gate,
  Borne by the joyous crowd.

LXV

They gave him of the corn-land,
  That was of public right,
As much as two strong oxen
  Could plow from morn till night;
And they made a molten image,
  And set it up on high,
And there it stands unto this day
  To witness if I lie.

---

[1] Hindrance.   [2] Deed.

LXVI

It stands in the Comitium,
　Plain for all folk to see,
Horatius in his harness,
　Halting ¹ upon one knee;
And underneath is written,
　In letters all of gold,
How valiantly he kept the bridge
　In the brave days of old.

LXVII

And still his name sounds stirring
　Unto the men of Rome,
As the trumpet-blast that cries to them
　To charge the Volscian home;
And wives still pray to Juno
　For boys with hearts as bold
As his who kept the bridge so well
　In the brave days of old.

LXVIII

And in the nights of winter,
　When the cold north winds blow,
And the long howling of the wolves
　Is heard amidst the snow;
When round the lonely cottage
　Roars loud the tempest's din,
And the good logs of Algidus
　Roar louder yet within;

LXIX

When the oldest cask ² is opened,
　And the largest lamp is lit;
When the chestnuts glow in the embers,
　And the kid ³ turns on the spit;

---

¹ Stooping.　　　² Cask of wine.　　　³ Young goat.

When young and old in circle
    Around the firebrands [1] close;
When the girls are weaving baskets, 580
    And the lads are shaping bows;

LXX

When the goodman [2] mends his armor,
    And trims his helmet's plume;
When the goodwife's shuttle merrily
    Goes flashing through the loom; 585
With weeping and with laughter
    Still is the story told,
How well Horatius kept the bridge
    In the brave days of old.

[1] Burning logs.   [2] Father of the family.

INTRODUCTION TO "THE BATTLE OF THE LAKE REGILLUS"

Macaulay, in his introduction to "The Battle of the Lake Regillus" makes the following points:
1. The poem is supposed to have been produced about ninety years after the lay of Horatius.
2. Some characters are common to each.
3. It has a slight tincture of Greek learning and of Greek superstition.
4. Images and incidents have been borrowed on principle from Homer's battle-pieces.
5. It was a popular belief from an early period that the battle was won through the supernatural agency of Castor and Pollux who fought in the battle, carried the news to Rome, washed their steeds at a well in the Forum, and disappeared. One of their horses left a hoof mark in the rock near Lake Regillus. In their honor a great festival was kept on the Ides of Quintilis.
6. The legend probably arose from the Roman general's vowing in the hour of peril, a temple to the Twin Gods, and further, from the statement by some man that he had seen godlike forms scattering the Latines.
7. When the equestrian order of Roman citizens was remodeled it was ordained that a grand muster and inspection of the order should be a part of the ceremony performed on the anniversary of the battle.
8. This poem is supposed to have been made for this great occasion.
9. Antiquaries differ widely as to the situation of the field of battle. The opinion of those who suppose that the armies met between Frascati and the Monte Porzio has been followed in this poem.

TLE OF THE LAKE REGILLUS

\T THE FEAST OF CASTOR AND POLLUX
N THE IDES OF QUINTILIS,
IE YEAR OF THE CITY CCCCLI

I

:ts, sound a war note!
rs, clear the way!
:s will ride, in all their pride,
e streets to-day.
doors and windows 5
with garlands all,
)r in the Forum,
without the wall.
it is robed in purple,
'e each is crowned; 10
ar horse under each
ightily the ground.
the Yellow River,
inds the Sacred Hill,
Ides of Quintilis 15
e such honor still.
Martian Kalends,
r's Nones are gay;
ud Ides, when the squadron [1] rides,
Rome's whitest day. 20

II

reat Twin Brethren
this solemn feast.
, the Great Twin Brethren
irring from the east.

[1] Knights on horseback.

They came o'er wild Parthenius
  Tossing in waves of pine,
O'er Cirrha's dome, o'er Adria's [1] foam,
  O'er purple Apennine,
From where with flutes and dances
  Their ancient mansion rings,
In lordly Lacedæmon,
  The city of two kings,
To where, by Lake Regillus,
  Under the Porcian height,
All in the lands of Tusculum,
  Was fought the glorious fight.

III

Now on the place of slaughter
  Are cots [2] and sheepfolds seen,
And rows of vines, and fields of wheat,
  And apple orchards green;
The swine crush the big acorns
  That fall from Corne's oaks;
Upon the turf by the Fair Fount
  The reaper's pottage [3] smokes.
The fisher baits his angle, [4]
  The hunter twangs his bow;
Little they think on those strong limbs
  That moulder deep below.
Little they think how sternly
  That day the trumpets pealed;
How in the slippery swamp of blood
  Warrior and war horse reeled;
How wolves came with fierce gallop,
  And crows on eager wings,
To tear the flesh of captains,
  And peck the eyes of kings;

---

[1] The Adriatic. [2] Huts. [3] Food. [4] Hook.

How thick the dead lay scattered
  Under the Porcian height;
How through the gates of Tusculum
  Raved the wild stream of flight;
And how the Lake Regillus
  Bubbled with crimson foam,
What time the Thirty Cities
  Came forth to war with Rome.

IV

But, Roman, when thou standest
  Upon that holy ground,
Look thou with heed on the dark rock
  That girds the dark lake round;
So shalt thou see a hoof mark
  Stamped deep into the flint;
It was no hoof of mortal steed
  That made so strange a dint.
There to the Great Twin Brethren
  Vow thou thy vows, and pray
That they, in tempest and in fight,
  Will keep thy head alway.

V

Since last the Great Twin Brethren
  Of mortal eyes were seen,
Have years gone by an hundred
  And fourscore and thirteen.
That summer a Virginius
  Was Consul first in place;
The second was stout [1] Aulus,
  Of the Posthumian race.

[1] Brave, resolute.

The Herald of the Latines
  From Gabii came in state;
The Herald of the Latines
  Passed through Rome's Eastern Gate;
The Herald of the Latines
  Did in our Forum stand,
And there he did his office,[1]
  A scepter [2] in his hand.

VI

"Hear, Senators and people
  Of the good town of Rome,
The Thirty Cities charge you
  To bring the Tarquins home;
And if ye still be stubborn,
  To work the Tarquins wrong,
The Thirty Cities warn you,
  Look that your walls be strong."

VII

Then spake the Consul Aulus—
  He spake a bitter jest—
"Once the jays sent a message
  Unto the eagle's nest:—
'Now yield thou up thine eyrie
  Unto the carrion kite,
Or come forth valiantly, and face
  The jays in deadly fight.'
Forth looked in wrath the eagle;
  And carrion kite and jay,
Soon as they saw his beak and claw
  Fled screaming far away."

---

[1] Duty.   [2] Symbol of office.

VIII

The Herald of the Latines
  Hath hied him back in state;
The Fathers of the City 115
  Are met in high debate.
Then spake the elder Consul,
  An ancient man and wise:
"Now hearken, Conscript Fathers,
  To that which I advise. 120
In seasons of great peril
  'Tis good that one bear sway;
Then choose we a Dictator,
  Whom all men shall obey.
Camerium knows how deeply 125
  The sword of Aulus bites,
And all our city calls him
  The man of seventy fights.
Then let him be Dictator
  For six months and no more, 130
And have a Master of the Knights
  And axes twenty-four."

IX

So Aulus was Dictator,
  The man of seventy fights;
He made Æbutius Elva 135
  His Master of the Knights.
On the third morn thereafter,
  At dawning of the day,
Did Aulus and Æbutius
  Set forth with their array. 140
Sempronius Atratinus
  Was left in charge at home
With boys, and with gray-headed men,
  To keep the walls of Rome.

Hard by the Lake Regillus
 Our camp was pitched at night;
Eastward a mile the Latines lay,
 Under the Porcian height.
Far over hill and valley
 Their mighty host was spread;
And with their thousand watch fires
 The midnight sky was red.

X

Up rose the golden morning
 Over the Porcian height,
The proud Ides of Quintilis
 Marked evermore with white.
Not without secret trouble
 Our bravest saw the foes;
For girt by threescore thousand spears
 The thirty standards rose.
From every warlike city
 That boasts the Latian name,
Foredoomed to dogs and vultures,
 That gallant army came:
From Setia's purple vineyards,
 From Norba's ancient wall,
From the white streets of Tusculum,
 The proudest town of all;
From where the Witch's Fortress
 O'erhangs the dark-blue seas;
From the still glassy lake that sleeps
 Beneath Aricia's trees—
Those trees in whose dim shadow
 The ghastly priest doth reign,
The priest who slew the slayer,
 And shall himself be slain;

From the drear banks of Ufens,
   Where flights of marsh fowl play,
And buffaloes lie wallowing
   Through the hot summer's day;
From the gigantic watch towers,
   No work of earthly men,
Whence Cora's sentinels o'erlook
   The never-ending fen;
From the Laurentian jungle,
   The wild hog's reedy home;
From the green steeps whence Anio leaps
   In floods of snow-white foam.

XI

Aricia, Cora, Norba,
   Velitræ, with the might
Of Setia and of Tusculum,
   Were marshaled on the right.
The leader was Mamilius,
   Prince of the Latian name;
Upon his head a helmet
   Of red gold shone like flame;
High on a gallant charger
   Of dark-gray hue he rode;
Over his gilded armor
   A vest of purple flowed,
Woven in the land of sunrise
   By Syria's dark-browed daughters,
And by the sails of Carthage brought
   Far o'er the southern waters.

XII

Lavinium and Laurentum
   Had on the left their post,
With all the banners of the marsh,
   And banners of the coast.

Their leader was false Sextus,
  That wrought the deed of shame;
With restless pace and haggard face
  To his last field he came.
Men said he saw strange visions
  Which none beside might see,
And that strange sounds were in his ears
  Which none might hear but he.
A woman fair and stately,
  But pale as are the dead,
Oft through the watches of the night
  Sat spinning by his bed.
And as she plied her distaff,
  In a sweet voice and low,
She sang of great old houses
  And fights fought long ago.
So spun she and so sang she,
  Until the east was gray,
Then pointed to her bleeding breast,
  And shrieked, and fled away.

XIII

But in the center thickest
  Were ranged the shields of foes,
And from the center loudest
  The cry of battle rose.
There Tibur marched and Pedum
  Beneath proud Tarquin's rule
And Ferentinum of the rock,
  And Gabii of the pool.
There rode the Volscian succors;
  There, in a dark stern ring,
The Roman exiles gathered close
  Around the ancient king.

Though white as Mount Soracte
  When winter nights are long,
His beard flowed down o'er mail and belt,
  His heart and hand were strong;
Under his hoary [1] eyebrows
  Still flashed forth quenchless rage,
And, if the lance shook in his gripe,
  'Twas more with hate than age.
Close at his side was Titus
  On an Apulian steed—
Titus, the youngest Tarquin,
  Too good for such a breed.

XIV

Now on each side the leaders
  Gave signal for the charge;
And on each side the footmen
  Strode on with lance and targe; [2]
And on each side the horsemen
  Struck their spurs deep in gore,
And front to front the armies
  Met with a mighty roar;
And under that great battle
  The earth with blood was red;
And, like the Pomptine fog at morn
  The dust hung overhead;
And louder still and louder
  Rose from the darkened field
The braying of the war horns,
  The clang of sword and shield,
The rush of squadrons sweeping
  Like whirlwinds o'er the plain,
The shouting of the slayers,
  And screeching of the slain.

[1] White.   [2] Shield.

XV

False Sextus rode out foremost,
　His look was high and bold;
His corselet [1] was of bison's [2] hide,
　Plated with steel and gold.
As glares the famished eagle
　From the Digentian rock
On a choice lamb that bounds alone
　Before Bandusia's flock,
Herminius glared on Sextus,
　And came with eagle speed,
Herminius on black Auster,
　Brave champion on brave steed;
In his right hand the broadsword
　That kept the bridge so well,
And on his helm [3] the crown he won
　When proud Fidenæ fell.
Woe to the maid whose lover
　Shall cross his path to-day!
False Sextus saw and trembled,
　And turned and fled away.
As turns, as flies, the woodman
　In the Calabrian brake,
When through the reeds gleams the round eye
　Of that fell speckled snake,
So turned, so fled, false Sextus,
　And hid him in the rear,
Behind the dark Lavinian ranks
　Bristling with crest and spear.

XVI

But far to the north Æbutius,
　The Master of the Knights,

---

[1] Armor for body.　　　[2] Wild ox.　　　[3] Helmet.

Gave Tubero of Norba
  To feed the Porcian kites.
Next under those red horsehoofs
  Flaccus of Setia lay;
Better had he been pruning
  Among his elms that day.
Mamilius saw the slaughter,
  And tossed his golden crest,
And towards the Master of the Knights
  Through the thick battle pressed.
Æbutius smote Mamilius
  So fiercely on the shield
That the great lord of Tusculum
  Well nigh rolled on the field.
Mamilius smote Æbutius,
  With a good aim and true,
Just where the neck and shoulder join,
  And pierced him through and through;
And brave Æbutius Elva
  Fell swooning to the ground,
But a thick wall of bucklers [1]
  Encompassed him around.
His clients from the battle
  Bare him some little space,
And filled a helm from the dark lake,
  And bathed his brow and face;
And when at last he opened
  His swimming eyes to light,
Men say, the earliest word he spake
  Was, "Friends, how goes the fight?"

XVII

But meanwhile in the center
  Great deeds of arms were wrought;

[1] Shields.

There Aulus the Dictator 335
  And there Valerius fought.
Aulus with his good broadsword
  A bloody passage cleared
To where, amidst the thickest foes,
  He saw the long white beard. 340
Flat lighted that good broadsword
  Upon proud Tarquin's head.
He dropped the lance, he dropped the reins;
  He fell as fall the dead.
Down Aulus springs to slay him, 345
  With eyes like coals of fire;
But faster Titus hath sprung down,
  And hath bestrode his sire.
Latian captains, Roman knights,
  Fast down to earth they spring, 350
And hand to hand they fight on foot
  Around the ancient king.
First Titus gave tall Cæso
  A death wound in the face;
Tall Cæso was the bravest man 355
  Of the brave Fabian race;[1]
Aulus slew Rex of Gabii,
  The priest of Juno's shrine;
Valerius smote down Julius,
  Of Rome's great Julian line— 360
Julius, who left his mansion
  High on the Velian hill,
And through all turns of weal and woe
  Followed proud Tarquin still.
Now right across proud Tarquin 365
  A corpse was Julius laid;
And Titus groaned with rage and grief,
  And at Valerius made.

[1] Family.

Valerius struck at Titus,
    And lopped off half his crest
But Titus stabbed Valerius
    A span deep in the breast.
Like a mast snapped by the tempest,
    Valerius reeled and fell.
Ah! woe is me for the good house
    That loves the people well!
Then shouted loud the Latines,
    And with one rush they bore
The struggling Romans backward
    Three lances' length and more;
And up they took proud Tarquin
    And laid him on a shield,
And four strong yeomen bare him,
    Still senseless, from the field.

XVIII

But fiercer grew the fighting
    Around Valerius dead;
For Titus dragged him by the foot
    And Aulus by the head.
"On, Latines, on!" quoth Titus,
    "See how the rebels fly!"
"Romans, stand firm!" quoth Aulus
    "And win this fight or die!
They must not give Valerius
    To raven and to kite;
For aye [1] Valerius loathed the wrong
    And aye upheld the right;
And for your wives and babies
    In the front rank he fell.
Now play the men for the good house
    That loves the people well!"

[1] Ever. Pronounced ā.

XIX

Then tenfold round the body
  The roar of battle rose,
Like the roar of a burning forest
  When a strong north wind blows.
Now backward and now forward   405
  Rocked furiously the fray,
Till none could see Valerius,
  And none wist [1] where he lay.
For shivered arms and ensigns
  Were heaped there in a mound,   410
And corpses stiff, and dying men
  That writhed and gnawed the ground;
And wounded horses kicking,
  And snorting purple foam;
Right well did such a couch befit   415
  A Consular of Rome.

XX

But north looked the Dictator;
  North looked he long and hard,
And spake to Caius Cossus,
  The Captain of his Guard: 420
"Caius, of all the Romans
  Thou hast the keenest sight;
Say, what through yonder storm of dust
  Comes from the Latian right?"

XXI

Then answered Caius Cossus: 425
  "I see an evil sight;
The banner of proud Tusculum
  Comes from the Latian right.
I see the plumed horsemen;
  And far before the rest   430

---
[1] Knew. Pret. of 'wit.'

I see the dark-gray charger,
   I see the purple vest,
I see the golden helmet
   That shines far off like flame;
So ever rides Mamilius
   Prince of the Latian name."

XXII

"Now hearken, Caius Cossus:
   Spring on thy horse's back;
Ride as [1] the wolves of Apennine
   Were all upon thy track;
Haste to our southward battle,
   And never draw thy rein
Until thou find Herminius,
   And bid him come amain."

XXIII

So Aulus spake, and turned him
   Again to that fierce strife;
And Caius Cossus mounted
   And rode for death and life.
Loud clanged beneath his horsehoofs
   The helmets of the dead,
And many a curdling pool of blood
   Splashed him from heel to head.
So came he far to southward,
   Where fought the Roman host,
Against the banners of the marsh
   And banners of the coast.
Like corn before the sickle
   The stout Lavinians fell,
Beneath the edge of the true sword
   That kept the bridge so well.

[1] As if.

XXIV

"Herminius! Aulus greets thee;
 He bids thee come with speed
To help our central battle,
 For sore is there our need.
There wars the youngest Tarquin
 And there the Crest of Flame,
The Tusculan Mamilius,
 Prince of the Latian name.
Valerius hath fallen fighting
 In front of our array,
And Aulus of the seventy fields
 Alone upholds the day."

XXV

Herminius beat his bosom,
 But never a word he spake.
He clapped his hand on Auster's mane,
 He gave the reins a shake;
Away, away went Auster
 Like an arrow from the bow—
Black Auster was the fleetest steed
 From Aufidus to Po.

XXVI

Right glad were all the Romans
 Who, in that hour of dread,
Against great odds bare up the war
 Around Valerius dead,
When from the south the cheering
 Rose with a mighty swell:
"Herminius comes, Herminius
 Who kept the bridge so well!"

XXVII

Mamilius spied Herminius
  And dashed across the way: 490
"Herminius! I have sought thee
  Through many a bloody day.
One of us two, Herminius,
  Shall never more go home.
I will lay on for Tusculum, 495
  And lay thou on for Rome!"

XXVIII

All round them paused the battle,
  While met in mortal fray
The Roman and the Tusculan,
  The horses black and gray. 500
Herminius smote Mamilius
  Through breastplate and through breast;
And fast flowed out the purple blood
  Over the purple vest.
Mamilius smote Herminius 505
  Through headpiece and through head;
And side by side those chiefs of pride
  Together fell down dead.
Down fell they dead together
  In a great lake of gore; 510
And still stood all who saw them fall
  While men might count a score.

XXIX

Fast, fast, with heels wild spurning,
  The dark-gray charger fled;
He burst through ranks of fighting men 515
  He sprang o'er heaps of dead.
His bridle far outstreaming,
  His flanks all blood and foam,

THE BATTLE OF THE LAKE REGILLUS

He sought the southern mountains,
    The mountains of his home.
The pass was steep and rugged,
    The wolves they howled and whined;
But he ran like a whirlwind up the pass,
    And he left the wolves behind.
Through many a startled hamlet
    Thundered his flying feet;
He rushed through the gates of Tusculum,
    He rushed up the long white street;
He rushed by tower and temple,
    And paused not from his race
Till he stood before his master's door
    In the stately market place.
And straightway round him gathered
    A pale and trembling crowd,
And when they knew him, cries of rage
    Brake forth, and wailing loud;
And women rent their tresses
    For their great prince's fall;
And old men girt on their old swords,
    And went to man the wall.

XXX

But, like a graven image,
    Black Auster kept his place,
And ever wistfully he looked
    Into his master's face.
The raven mane that daily,
    With pats and fond caresses,
The young Herminia washed and combed,
    And twined in even tresses,
And decked with colored ribbons
    From her own gay attire,
Hung sadly o'er her father's corpse

In carnage and in mire.
Forth with a shout sprang Titus
  And seized black Auster's rein.
Then Aulus sware a fearful oath, 555
  And ran at him amain:
"The furies of thy brother
  With me and mine abide,
If one of your accursed house
  Upon black Auster ride!" 560
As on an Alpine watchtower
  From heaven comes down the flame,
Full on the neck of Titus
  The blade of Aulus came;
And out the red blood spouted 565
  In a wide arch and tall,
As spouts a fountain in the court
  Of some rich Capuan's hall.
The knees of all the Latines
  Were loosened with dismay 570
When dead, on dead Herminius
  The bravest Tarquin lay.

XXXI

And Aulus the Dictator
  Stroked Auster's raven mane,
With heed he looked unto the girths, 575
  With heed unto the rein.
"Now bear me well, black Auster,
  Unto yon thick array,
And thou and I will have revenge
  For thy good lord this day." 580

XXXII

So spake he, and was buckling
  Tighter black Auster's band,

When he was aware of a princely pair
  That rode at his right hand.
So like they were, no mortal
  Might one from other know;
White as snow their armor was,
  Their steeds were white as snow.
Never on earthly anvil
  Did such rare armor gleam,
And never did such gallant steeds
  Drink of an earthly stream.

XXXIII

And all who saw them trembled,
  And pale grew every cheek;
And Aulus the Dictator
  Scarce gathered voice to speak:
"Say by what name men call you?
  What city is your home?
And wherefore ride ye in such guise
  Before the ranks of Rome?"

XXXIV

"By many names men call us,
  In many lands we dwell:
Well Samothracia knows us,
  Cyrene knows us well;
Our house in gay Tarentum
  Is hung each morn with flowers;
High o'er the masts of Syracuse
  Our marble portal[1] towers;
But by the proud Eurotas
  Is our dear native home;
And for the right we come to fight
  Before the ranks of Rome."

[1] Doorway of their temple.

XXXV

So answered those strange horsemen,
    And each couched [1] low his spear;
And forthwith all the ranks of Rome　　　　615
    Were bold and of good cheer;
And on the thirty armies
    Came wonder and affright,
And Ardea wavered on the left,
    And Cora on the right.　　　　620
"Rome to the charge!" cried Aulus;
    "The foe begins to yield!
Charge for the hearth of Vesta!
    Charge for the Golden Shield!
Let no man stop to plunder,　　　　625
    But slay, and slay, and slay;
The gods who live forever
    Are on our side to-day."

XXXVI

Then the fierce trumpet flourish
    From earth to heaven arose.　　　　630
The kites know well the long stern swell
    That bids the Romans close.[2]
Then the good sword of Aulus
    Was lifted up to slay;
Then like a crag down Apennine　　　　635
    Rushed Auster through the fray.
But under those strange horsemen
    Still thicker lay the slain;
And after those strange horses
    Black Auster toiled in vain.　　　　640
Behind them Rome's long battle [3]

[1] Leveled.　　　[2] Come to close quarters.　　　[3] Line of battle.

Came rolling on the foe,
Ensigns dancing wild above,
  Blades all in line below.
So comes the Po in flood time
  Upon the Celtic plain;
So comes the squall, blacker than night,
  Upon the Adrian main.
Now, by our Sire Quirinus,
  It was a goodly sight
To see the thirty standards
  Swept down the tide of flight.
So flies the spray of Adria
  When the black squall doth blow;
So corn sheaves in the flood time
  Spin down the whirling Po.
False Sextus to the mountains
  Turned first his horse's head;
And fast fled Ferentinum,
  And fast Lanuvium fled.
The horsemen of Nomentum
  Spurred hard out of the fray;
The footmen of Velitræ
  Threw shield and spear away.
And underfoot was trampled,
  Amidst the mud and gore,
The banner of proud Tusculum,
  That never stooped before;
And down went Flavius Faustus,
  Who led his stately ranks
From where the apple blossoms wave
  On Anio's echoing banks;
And Tullus of Arpinum,
  Chief of the Volscian aids,
And Metius with the long fair curls,
  The love of Anxur's maids,

And the white head of Vulso,
    The great Arician seer,
And Nepos of Laurentum,
    The hunter of the deer;
And in the back false Sextus
    Felt the good Roman steel,
And wriggling in the dust he died,
    Like a worm beneath the wheel;
And fliers and pursuers
    Were mingled in a mass;
And far away the battle
    Went roaring through the pass.

XXXVII

Sempronius Atratinus
    Sate in the Eastern Gate,
Beside him were three Fathers,
    Each in his chair of state—
Fabius, whose nine stout grandsons
    That day were in the field,
And Manlius, eldest of the Twelve
    Who kept the Golden Shield,
And Sergius, the High Pontiff,
    For wisdom far renowned;
In all Etruria's colleges
    Was no such Pontiff found.
And all around the portal,
    And high above the wall,
Stood a great throng of people,
    But sad and silent all;
Young lads and stooping elders
    That might not bear the mail,[1]
Matrons with lips that quivered,
    And maids with faces pale.

[1] Armor.

Since the first gleam of daylight,
  Sempronius had not ceased
To listen for the rushing
  Of horsehoofs from the east.
The mist of eve was rising,
  The sun was hastening down,
When he was aware of a princely pair
  Fast pricking towards the town.
So like they were, man never
  Saw twins so like before;
Red with gore their armor was,
  Their steeds were red with gore.

XXXVIII
"Hail to the great Asylum!
  Hail to the hilltops seven!
Hail·to the fire that burns for aye,
  And the shield that fell from heaven!
This day, by Lake Regillus,
  Under the Porcian height,
All in the lands of Tusculum
  Was fought a glorious fight.
To-morrow your Dictator
  Shall bring in triumph home
The spoils of thirty cities
  To deck the shrines of Rome!"

XXXIX
Then burst from that great concourse
  A shout that shook the towers,
And some ran north, and some ran south,
  Crying, "The day is ours!"
But on rode these strange horsemen
  With slow and lordly pace,
And none who saw their bearing
  Durst ask their name or race.

On rode they to the Forum,
  While laurel boughs and flowers,
From housetops and from windows,
  Fell on their crests in showers.
When they drew nigh to Vesta,
  They vaulted down amain,
And washed their horses in the well
  That springs by Vesta's fane.[1]
And straight again they mounted,
  And rode to Vesta's door;
Then, like a blast, away they passed,
  And no man saw them more.

XL

And all the people trembled,
  And pale grew every cheek;
And Sergius the High Pontiff
  Alone found voice to speak:
"The gods who live for ever
  Have fought for Rome to-day!
These be the Great Twin Brethren
  To whom the Dorians pray.
Back comes the Chief in triumph
  Who in the hour of fight
Hath seen the Great Twin Brethren
  In harness on his right.
Safe comes the ship to haven,
  Through billows and through gales,
If once the Great Twin Brethren
  Sit shining on their sails.
Wherefore they washed their horses
  In Vesta's holy well,
Wherefore they rode to Vesta's door,
  I know, but may not tell.

[1] Shrine.

Here, hard by Vesta's Temple,
  Build we a stately dome
Unto the Great Twin Brethren
  Who fought so well for Rome.
And when the months returning
  Bring back this day of fight,
The proud Ides of Quintilis,
  Marked evermore with white,
Unto the Great Twin Brethren
  Let all the people throng,
With chaplets and with offerings,
  With music and with song;
And let the doors and windows
  Be hung with garlands all,
And let the Knights be summoned
  To Mars without the wall;
Thence let them ride in purple
  With joyous trumpet sound,
Each mounted on his war horse,
  And each with olive crowned;
And pass in solemn order
  Before the sacred dome,
Where dwell the Great Twin Brethren
  Who fought so well for Rome!"

INTRODUCTION TO "VIRGINIA"

Macaulay, in his introduction to "Virginia", makes the following points:

1. A collection consisting exclusively of war songs would give an imperfect, or rather an erroneous, notion of the spirit of the old Latin ballads, for the war songs dealt only with Patrician or upper class heroes.
2. But there was a class of compositions in which the great houses were by no means so courteously treated. These dealt with those parts of early Roman history which relate to the long contest between the great families of the Patricians and the commonalty or Plebeians.
3. The Plebeians suffered under many grievances: particularly, their exclusion from the highest magistracies; their exclusion from all share in the public lands; and the hard laws of debtor and creditor.
4. But the Plebeians had secured some constitutional rights. They had secured representation by Tribunes who, though they had no share in the government, could safeguard the people. And the people had gradually wrung other concessions from the aristocracy.
5. In A. U. C. 378 the Tribune, Caius Licinius, seconded by his colleague, Lucius Sextius, proposed the three Licinian laws to redress the three grievances. Being elected year after year, finally they won. The result was a united city which became the mistress of the world.
6. During the great Licinian contest the Plebeian poets were, doubtless, not silent. And songs are powerful at such times. These songs are satirical poems. This was a

native form of composition in which the Latin literature excels.
7. These minstrels appear generally to have taken the popular side. Doubtless they versified the speeches of the Tribunes and heaped abuse on the leaders of the aristocracy dwelling on every personal defect, domestic scandal, and dishonorable tradition.
8. During the Licinian conflict a fierce opponent of the Plebeians was Appius Claudius Crassus whose line offered a shining mark for the satirists as its history was noted for cowardice and arrogance. His grandfather called by the same name was as detested as Sextus Tarquinius for, during a crisis, not only had he secured the abolition of the Tribuneship and the establishment of a Council of Ten, called Decemvirs, but his administration had been swept away as a result of an attempted outrage upon a beautiful young girl of humble birth.
9. This story was doubtless seized upon by the minstrels.
10. "In order that the reader may judge fairly of these fragments of the lay of Virginia, he must imagine himself a Plebeian who has just voted for the reëlection of Sextius and Licinius. All the power of the Patricians has been exerted to throw out the two great champions of the Commons. Every Posthumius, Æmilius, and Cornelius has used his influence to the utmost. Debtors have been let out of the workhouses on condition of voting against the men of the people; clients have been posted to hiss and to interrupt the favorite candidates; Appius Claudius Crassus has spoken with more than his usual eloquence and asperity; all has been in vain; Licinius and Sextius have a fifth time carried all the tribes; work is suspended; the booths are closed; the Plebeians bear on their shoulders the two champions of liberty through the Forum. Just at this moment it is announced that a popular poet, a zealous adherent of the Tribunes, has made a new song

which will cut the Claudian nobles to the heart. The crowd gathers round him, and calls on him to recite it. He takes his stand on the spot where, according to tradition, Virginia, more than seventy years ago, was seized by the pander of Appius, and he begins his story."

VIRGINIA

FRAGMENTS OF A LAY SUNG IN THE FORUM ON THE DAY WHEREON LUCIUS SEXTIUS SEXTINUS LATERANUS AND CAIUS LICINIUS CALVUS STOLO WERE ELECTED TRIBUNES OF THE COMMONS THE FIFTH TIME, IN THE YEAR OF THE CITY CCCLXXXII [1]

Ye good men of the Commons, with loving hearts and true,
Who stand by the bold Tribunes that still have stood by you,
Come, make a circle round me, and mark my tale with care,—
A tale of what once Rome hath borne, of what Rome yet may bear.
This is no Grecian fable,[2] of fountains running wine, 5
Of maids with snaky tresses, or sailors turned to swine.
Here, in this very Forum, under the noonday sun,
In sight of all the people, the bloody deed was done.
Old men still creep among us who saw that fearful day,
Just seventy years and seven ago, when the wicked Ten bare sway. 10

Of all the wicked Ten still the names are held accursed,
And of all the wicked Ten Appius Claudius was the worst.
He stalked along the Forum like King Tarquin in his pride;
Twelve axes waited on him, six marching on a side.
The townsmen shrank to right and left, and eyed askance with fear 15
His lowering brow, his curling mouth, which always seemed to sneer.
That brow of hate, that mouth of scorn, marks all the kindred still;
For never was there Claudius yet but wished the Commons ill.

[1] B. C. 372.   [2] Myth.

Nor lacks he fit attendance; for close behind his heels,
With outstretched chin and crouching pace, the client Marcus steals, 20
His loins girt up to run with speed, be the errand what it may,
And the smile flickering on his cheek for aught his lord may say.
Such varlets pimp and jest for hire among the lying Greeks;
Such varlets still are paid to hoot when brave Licinius speaks.
Where'er ye shed the honey, the buzzing flies will crowd; 25
Where'er ye fling the carrion, the raven's croak is loud;
Where'er down Tiber garbage floats, the greedy pike ye see;
And wheresoe'er such lord is found, such client still will be.

   Just then, as through one cloudless chink in a black and stormy sky
Shines out the dewy morning-star, a fair young girl came by. 30
With her small tablets in her hand and her satchel on her arm,
Home she went bounding from the school, nor dreamed of shame or harm;
And past those dreaded axes she innocently ran,
With bright, frank brow that had not learned to blush at gaze of man;
And up the Sacred Street she turned, and, as she danced along, 35
She warbled gayly to herself lines of the good old song,
How for a sport the princes came spurring from the camp,
And found Lucrece combing the fleece under the midnight lamp.
The maiden sang as sings the lark, when up he darts his flight,
From his nest in the green April corn, to meet the morning light;
And Appius heard her sweet young voice, and saw her sweet young face, 41
And loved her with the accursed love of his accursed race,
And all along the Forum and up the Sacred Street,
His vulture eye pursued the trip of those small glancing feet.

   *   *   *   *   *   *   *   *   *   *

VIRGINIA

Over the Alban mountains the light of morning broke;　45
From all the roofs of the Seven Hills curled the thin wreaths of smoke;
The city gates were opened; the Forum, all alive
With buyers and with sellers, was humming like a hive;
Blithely on brass and timber the craftsman's stroke was ringing,
And blithely o'er her panniers [1] the market girl was singing,　50
And blithely young Virginia came smiling from her home;
Ah! woe for young Virginia, the sweetest maid in Rome!
With her small tablets in her hand and her satchel on her arm,
Forth she went bounding to the school, nor dreamed of shame or harm.
She crossed the Forum shining with stalls [2] in alleys gay,　55
And just had reached the very spot whereon I stand this day,
When up the varlet Marcus came; not such as when erewhile
He crouched behind his patron's heels with the true client smile;
He came with lowering forehead, swollen features, and clenched fist,
And strode across Virginia's path, and caught her by the wrist.　60
Hard strove the frightened maiden and screamed with look aghast,
And at her scream from right and left the folk came running fast,—
The money changer Crispus, with his thin silver hairs,
And Hanno from the stately booth glittering with Punic [3] wares,
And the strong smith Muræna, grasping a half-forged brand,　65
And Volero the flesher,[4] his cleaver in his hand.
All came in wrath and wonder, for all knew that fair child,
And, as she passed them twice a day, all kissed their hands and smiled;
And the strong smith Muræna gave Marcus such a blow,
The caitiff reeled three paces back, and let the maiden go.　70
Yet glared he fiercely round him, and growled in harsh, fell tone,
"She's mine, and I will have her; I seek but for mine own.

[1] Baskets.　　[2] Small shops.　　[3] Carthaginian.　　[4] Butcher.

She is my slave, born in my house, and stolen away and sold,
The year of the sore sickness, ere she was twelve hours old.
'Twas in the sad September, the month of wail and fright; 75
Two augurs were borne forth that morn, the Consul died ere night.
I wait on Appius Claudius, I waited on his sire;
Let him who works the client wrong beware the patron's ire!"

So spake the varlet Marcus; and dread and silence came
On all the people at the sound of the great Claudian name. 80
For then there was no Tribune to speak the word of might,
Which makes the rich man tremble, and guards the poor man's right.
There was no brave Licinius, no honest Sextius then;
But all the city, in great fear, obeyed the wicked Ten.
Yet ere the varlet Marcus again might seize the maid, 85
Who clung tight to Muræna's skirt and sobbed and shrieked for aid,
Forth through the throng of gazers the young Icilius pressed,
And stamped his foot, and rent his gown, and smote upon his breast,
And sprang upon that column, by many a minstrel sung,
Whereon three moldering helmets, three rusting swords, are hung, 90
And beckoned to the people, and in bold voice and clear
Poured thick and fast the burning words which tyrants quake to hear:

"Now, by your children's cradles, now by your fathers' graves,
Be men to-day, Quirites, or be forever slaves!
For this did Servius give us laws? For this did Lucrece bleed? 95
For this was the great vengeance wrought on Tarquin's evil seed?[1]

[1] Posterity.

For this did those false sons make red the axes of their sire?
For this did Scævola's right hand hiss in the Tuscan fire?
Shall the vile fox-earth awe the race that stormed the lion's den?
Shall we, who could not brook one lord, crouch to the wicked Ten? 100
O for that ancient spirit which curbed the Senate's will!
O for the tents which in old time whitened the Sacred Hill!
In those brave days our fathers stood firmly side by side;
They faced the Marcian fury, they tamed the Fabian pride;
They drove the fiercest Quinctius an outcast forth from Rome; 105
They sent the haughtiest Claudius with shivered fasces home.
But what their care bequeathed us our madness flung away;
All the ripe fruit of threescore years was blighted in a day.
Exult, ye proud Patricians! The hard-fought fight is o'er.
We strove for honors—'twas in vain; for freedom—'tis no more. 110
No crier to the polling summons the eager throng;
No tribune breathes the word of might that guards the weak from wrong.
Our very hearts, that were so high, sink down beneath your will.
Riches and lands, and power and state—ye have them; keep them still.
Still keep the holy fillets; still keep the purple gown, 115
The axes and the curule chair, the car and laurel crown;
Still press us for your cohorts, and, when the fight is done,
Still fill your garners from the soil which our good swords have won.
Still, like a spreading ulcer which leech-craft [1] may not cure,
Let your foul usance eat away the substance [2] of the poor. 120
Still let your haggard debtors bear all their fathers bore;
Still let your dens of torment be noisome as of yore;
No fire when Tiber freezes; no air in dog-star heat;
And store of rods for free-born backs, and holes for free-born feet.

[1] Medical skill. [2] Possessions.

Heap heavier still the fetters, bar closer still the grate; [1] 125
Patient as sheep we yield us up unto your cruel hate.
But, by the Shades beneath us, and by the Gods above,
Add not unto your cruel hate your yet more cruel love!
Have ye not graceful ladies, whose spotless lineage springs
From Consuls and High Pontiffs and ancient Alban Kings? 130
Ladies, who deign not on our paths to set their tender feet,
Who from their cars look down with scorn upon the wondering street,
Who in Corinthian mirrors their own proud smiles behold,
And breathe of Capuan odors, and shine with Spanish gold?
Then leave the poor Plebeian his single tie to life— 135
The sweet, sweet love of daughter, of sister, and of wife,
The gentle speech, the balm for all that his vexed soul endures,
The kiss, in which he half forgets even such a yoke as yours.
Still let the maiden's beauty swell the father's breast with pride;
Still let the bridegroom's arms infold an unpolluted bride. 140
Spare us the inexpiable wrong, the unutterable shame,
That turns the coward's heart to steel, the sluggard's blood to flame,
Lest, when our latest hope is fled, ye taste of our despair,
And learn by proof, in some wild hour, how much the wretched dare."

* * * * * * * * * *

Straightway Virginius led the maid a little space aside, 145
To where the reeking shambles [2] stood, piled up with horn and hide,
Close to yon low dark archway, where in a crimson flood
Leaps down to the great sewer the gurgling stream of blood.
Hard by, a flesher on a block had laid his whittle [3] down;
Virginius caught the whittle up and hid it in his gown. 150
And then his eyes grew very dim, and his throat began to swell,
And in a hoarse, changed voice he spake, "Farewell, sweet child! Farewell!

[1] The bars.   [2] Slaughterhouses.   [3] Knife.

O how I loved my darling! Though stern I sometimes be,
To thee thou know'st I was not so. Who could be so to thee?
And how my darling loved me! How glad she was to hear 155
My footstep on the threshold when I came back last year!
And how she danced with pleasure to see my civic crown,
And took my sword and hung it up, and brought me forth my gown!
Now, all those things are over—yes, all thy pretty ways,
Thy needlework, thy prattle, thy snatches of old lays; 160
And none will grieve when I go forth, or smile when I return,
Or watch beside the old man's bed, or weep·upon his urn.
The house that was the happiest within the Roman walls,
The house that envied not the wealth of Capua's marble halls,
Now, for the brightness of thy smile, must have eternal gloom, 165
And for the music of thy voice, the silence of the tomb.
The time is come. See how he points his eager hand this way!
See how his eyes gloat on thy grief, like a kite's upon the prey!
With all his wit, he little deems that, spurned, betrayed, bereft,
Thy father hath in his despair one fearful refuge left. 170
He little deems that in this hand I clutch what still can save
Thy gentle youth from taunts and blows, the portion of the slave;
Yea, and from nameless evil, that passeth taunt and blow—
Foul outrage which thou knowest not, which thou shalt never know.
Then clasp me round the neck once more, and give me one more kiss; 175
And now, mine own dear little girl, there is no way but this."
With that he lifted high the steel and smote her in the side,
And in her blood she sank to earth, and with one sob she died.

Then, for a little moment, all people held their breath,
And through the crowded Forum was stillness as of death; 180
And in another moment brake forth from one and all
A cry as if the Volscians were coming o'er the wall.

Some with averted faces shrieking fled home amain;
Some ran to call a leech, [1] and some ran to lift the slain;
Some felt her lips and little wrist, if life might there be found; 185
And some tore up their garments fast, and strove to stanch the wound.
In vain they ran and felt and stanched; for never truer blow
That good right arm had dealt in fight against a Volscian foe.

When Appius Claudius saw that deed, he shuddered and sank down,
And hid his face some little space with the corner of his gown, 190
Till with white lips and bloodshot eyes, Virginius tottered nigh,
And stood before the judgment seat, and held the knife on high.
"O dwellers in the nether gloom, avengers of the slain,
By this dear blood I cry to you, do right between us twain;
And even as Appius Claudius hath dealt by me and mine, 195
Deal you by Appius Claudius and all the Claudian line!"
So spake the slayer of his child, and turned and went his way;
But first he cast one haggard glance to where the body lay,
And writhed, and groaned a fearful groan, and then with steadfast feet
Strode right across the market place unto the Sacred Street. 200

Then up sprang Appius Claudius: "Stop him, alive or dead!
Ten thousand pounds of copper to the man who brings his head."
He looked upon his clients, but none would work his will;
He looked upon his lictors, but they trembled and stood still.
And, as Virginius through the press [2] his way in silence cleft, 205
Ever the mighty multitude fell back to right and left.
And he hath passed in safety unto his woeful home,
And there ta'en horse to tell the camp what deeds are done in Rome.

[1] Physician.   [2] Throng.

VIRGINIA

By this the flood of people was swollen from every side,
And streets and porches [1] round were filled with that o'erflow-
   ing tide;
And close around the body gathered a little train
Of them that were the nearest and dearest to the slain.
They brought a bier, and hung it with many a cypress crown,
And gently they uplifted her, and gently laid her down.
The face of Appius Claudius wore the Claudian scowl and sneer,
And in the Claudian note [2] he cried, "What doth this rabble here?
Have they no crafts [3] to mind at home, that hitherward they
   stray?
Ho! lictors, clear the market place, and fetch the corpse away!"
The voice of grief and fury till then had not been loud;
But a deep sullen murmur wandered among the crowd,
Like the moaning noise that goes before the whirlwind on the
   deep,
Or the growl of a fierce watch dog but half-aroused from sleep.
But when the lictors at that word, tall yeomen [4] all and strong,
Each with his ax and sheaf of twigs, went down into the throng,
Those old men say, who saw that day of sorrow and of sin,
That in the Roman Forum was never such a din.
The wailing, hooting, cursing, the howls of grief and hate,
Were heard beyond the Pincian Hill, beyond the Latin Gate.
But close around the body, where stood the little train
Of them that were the nearest and dearest to the slain,
No cries were there, but teeth set fast, low whispers and black
   frowns,
And breaking up of benches and girding up of gowns.
'Twas well the lictors might not pierce to where the maiden lay,
Else surely had they been all twelve torn limb from limb that day.
Right glad they were to struggle back, blood streaming from
   their heads,
With axes all in splinters, and raiment all in shreds.

[1] Covered walks.
[2] Manner of speaking.
[3] Trades, occupation, business.
[4] Guards.

Then Appius Claudius gnawed his lip, and the blood left his
    cheek,
And thrice he beckoned with his hand, and thrice he strove to
    speak,
And thrice the tossing Forum set up a frightful yell:
"See, see, thou dog! what thou hast done, and hide thy shame
    in hell! 240
Thou that wouldst make our maidens slaves must first make
    slaves of men.
Tribunes! Hurrah for Tribunes! Down with the wicked Ten!"
And straightway, thick as hailstones, came whizzing through
    the air
Pebbles and bricks and potsherds all round the curule chair;
And upon Appius Claudius great fear and trembling came, 245
For never was a Claudius yet brave against aught but shame.
Though the great houses love us not, we own, to do them
    right,
That the great houses, all save one, have borne them well in
    fight.
Still Caius of Corioli, his triumphs and his wrongs,
His vengeance and his mercy, live in our camp-fire songs. 250
Beneath the yoke of Furius oft have Gaul and Tuscan bowed;
And Rome may bear the pride of him of whom herself is proud.
But evermore a Claudius shrinks from a stricken field,
And changes color like a maid at sight of sword and shield.
The Claudian triumphs all were won within the city towers; 255
The Claudian yoke was never pressed on any neck but ours.
A Cossus, like a wild cat, springs ever at the face;
A Fabius rushes like a boar against the shouting chase;
But the vile Claudian litter, raging with currish spite,
Still yelps and snaps at those who run, still runs from those who
    smite. 260
So now 'twas seen of Appius. When stones began to fly,
He shook and crouched, and wrung his hands, and smote upon
    his thigh:

"Kind clients, honest lictors, stand by me in this fray!
Must I be torn in pieces? Home, home, the nearest way!"
While yet he spake, and looked around with a bewildered stare, 265
Four sturdy lictors put their necks beneath the curule chair;
And fourscore clients on the left and fourscore on the right
Arrayed themselves with swords and staves, and loins girt up for fight.
But, though without or [1] staff or sword, so furious was the throng,
That scarce the train with might and main could bring their lord along. 270
Twelve times the crowd made at him, five times they seized his gown;
Small chance was his to rise again, if once they got him down;
And sharper came the pelting, and evermore the yell—
"Tribunes! We will have Tribunes!"—rose with a louder swell;
And the chair tossed as tosses a bark with tattered sail 275
When raves the Adriatic beneath an eastern gale,
When the Calabrian sea-marks are lost in clouds of spume,[2]
And the great Thunder Cape has donned his veil of inky gloom.
One stone hit Appius in the mouth, and one beneath the ear,
And ere he reached Mount Palatine he swooned with pain and fear. 280
His cursed head, that he was wont to hold so high with pride,
Now, like a drunken man's, hung down and swayed from side to side;
And when his stout retainers had brought him to his door,
His face and neck were all one cake of filth and clotted gore.
As Appius Claudius was that day, so may his grandson be! 285
God send Rome one such other sight, and send me there to see!

* * * * * * * * * *

[1] Poetical for "either."   [2] Foam.

INTRODUCTION TO "THE PROPHECY OF CAPYS"

Macaulay, in his introduction to "The Prophecy of Capys", makes the following points:
1. Romulus, after he had slain his granduncle Amulius, and restored his grandfather Numitor, determined to quit Alba, the hereditary domain of the Sylvian princes, and to found a new city.
2. This event was likely to be a favorite theme of the old Latin minstrels, who would attribute the project to divine intimation of the destined power of the city and who would introduce seers foretelling victories especially the last great one.
3. There is nothing strange in the supposition that the poet who was employed to celebrate the first great triumph of the Romans over the Greeks might throw his song of exultation into this form.
4. The occasion was one likely to excite the strongest feelings of national pride. Lucius Posthumius Megellus had been sent for the purpose of demanding reparation for injuries to Tarentum where he had been insulted, his gown being bespattered with filth. Declaring that "it will take not a little blood to wash this gown," he returned home. Rome declared war. Despite Pyrrhus' army and elephants sent to help the Greeks, despite their fame in arms they were defeated by the Romans. Manius Curius Dentatus, the successful general, received a great triumph in the city.
5. On such a day of triumphal procession the patriotic enthusiasm of a Latin poet would vent itself, admitting the superiority of the Greeks in the lazy arts of peace but boasting of the Roman preëminence in all the qualities which fit a people to subdue and to govern mankind.

6. The following lay belongs to the latest age of Latin ballad poetry. The minstrel's poem shows a much wider acquaintance with the geography, manners, and productions of remote nations than would have been found in the compositions of an earlier age. The poet troubles himself little about dates and introduces the things spoken of by travelers without thought of inquiring whether these things existed in the age of Romulus.

THE PROPHECY OF CAPYS

A LAY SUNG AT THE BANQUET IN THE CAPITOL, ON THE DAY WHEREON MANIUS CURIUS DENTATUS, A SECOND TIME CONSUL, TRIUMPHED OVER KING PYRRHUS AND THE TARENTINES, IN THE YEAR OF THE CITY CCCCLXXIX[1]

I

Now slain is King Amulius,
  Of the great Sylvian line,
Who reigned in Alba Longa,
  On the throne of Aventine.
Slain is the Pontiff Camers,
  Who spake the words of doom:
"The children to the Tiber;
  The mother to the tomb."

II

In Alba's lake no fisher
  His net to-day is flinging;
On the dark rind of Alba's oaks
  To-day no ax is ringing;
The yoke hangs o'er the manger,
  The scythe lies in the hay;
Through all the Alban villages
  No work is done to-day.

III

And every Alban burgher
  Hath donned his whitest gown;
And every head in Alba
  Weareth a poplar crown;

[1] B. C. 275.

And every Alban doorpost
    With boughs and flowers is gay;
For to-day the dead are living,
    The lost are found to-day.

IV

They were doomed by a bloody king,
    They were doomed by a lying priest;
They were cast on the raging flood,
    They were tracked by the raging beast.
Raging beast and raging flood
    Alike have spared their prey;
And to-day the dead are living,
    The lost are found to-day.

V

The troubled river knew them
    And smoothed his yellow foam,
And gently rocked the cradle
    That bore the fate of Rome.
The ravening she-wolf knew them
    And licked them o'er and o'er,
And gave them of her own fierce milk,
    Rich with raw flesh and gore.
Twenty winters, twenty springs,
    Since then have rolled away;
And to-day the dead are living,
    The lost are found to-day.

VI

Blithe it was to see the twins,
    Right goodly youths and tall,
Marching from Alba Longa
    To their old grandsire's hall.

Along their path fresh garlands
  Are hung from tree to tree;
Before them stride the pipers,
  Piping a note of glee.

VII

On the right goes Romulus
  With arms to the elbows red,
And in his hand a broadsword
  And on the blade a head—
A head in an iron helmet,
  With horsehair hanging down,
A shaggy head, a swarthy head,
  Fixed in a ghastly frown—
The head of King Amulius
  Of the great Sylvian line,
Who reigned in Alba Longa
  On the throne of Aventine.

VIII

On the left side goes Remus
  With wrists and fingers red,
And in his hand a boar-spear,
  And on the point a head—
A wrinkled head and aged,
  With silver beard and hair,
And holy fillets round it,
  Such as the pontiffs wear—
The head of ancient Camers,
  Who spake the words of doom:
"The children to the Tiber;
  The mother to the tomb."

IX

Two and two behind the twins
  Their trusty comrades go,

THE PROPHECY OF CAPYS

Four and forty valiant men,
  With club and ax and bow.
On each side every hamlet
  Pours forth its joyous crowd,
Shouting lads and baying dogs
  And children laughing loud,
And old men weeping fondly
  As Rhea's boys go by,
And maids who shriek to see the heads,
  Yet shrieking, press more nigh.

X

So they marched along the lake;
  They marched by fold and stall,
By cornfield and by vineyard,
  Unto the old man's hall.

XI

In the hall-gate sate Capys,
  Capys, the sightless seer;
From head to foot he trembled
  As Romulus drew near.
And up stood stiff his thin white hair,
  And his blind eyes flashed fire:
"Hail! foster child of the wondrous nurse!
  Hail! son of the wondrous sire!

XII

"But thou—What dost thou here
  In the old man's peaceful hall?
What doth the eagle in the coop,
  The bison in the stall?
Our corn fills many a garner,
  Our vines clasp many a tree,
Our flocks are white on many a hill,
  But these are not for thee.

XIII

"For thee no treasure ripens
  In the Tartessian mine;
For thee no ship brings precious bales
  Across the Libyan brine;
Thou shalt not drink from amber,
  Thou shalt not rest on down;
Arabia shall not steep thy locks,
  Nor Sidon tinge thy gown.

XIV

"Leave gold and myrrh and jewels,
  Rich table and soft bed,
To them who of man's seed are born,
  Whom woman's milk hath fed.
Thou wast not made for lucre,
  For pleasure, nor for rest;
Thou, that art sprung from the War-god's [1] loins,
  And hast tugged at the she-wolf's breast.

XV

"From sunrise unto sunset
  All earth shall hear thy fame;
A glorious city thou shalt build,
  And name it by thy name;
And there, unquenched through ages,
  Like Vesta's sacred fire,
Shall live the spirit of thy nurse,
  The spirit of thy sire.

XVI

"The ox toils through the furrow,
  Obedient to the goad;
The patient ass, up flinty paths,
  Plods with his weary load;

[1] Mars.

THE PROPHECY OF CAPYS

With whine and bound the spaniel
    His master's whistle hears;
And the sheep yields her patiently
    To the loud clashing shears.

XVII

"But thy nurse will hear no master,
    Thy nurse will bear no load;
And woe to them that shear her,
    And woe to them that goad!
When all the pack,[1] loud baying,
    Her bloody lair surrounds,
She dies in silence, biting hard,
    Amidst the dying hounds.

XVIII

"Pomona loves the orchard,
    And Liber loves the vine,
And Pales loves the straw-built shed
    Warm with the breath of kine;
And Venus loves the whispers
    Of plighted youth and maid,
In April's ivory moonlight
    Beneath the chestnut shade.

XIX

"But thy father loves the clashing
    Of broadsword and of shield;
He loves to drink the steam that reeks
    From the fresh battlefield;
He smiles a smile more dreadful
    Than his own dreadful frown,
When he sees the thick black cloud of smoke
    Go up from the conquered town.

[1] Of hounds.

XX

"And such as is the War-god,
    The author of thy line,
And such as she who suckled thee,
    Even such be thou and thine.
Leave to the soft Campanian
    His baths and his perfumes;
Leave to the sordid race of Tyre
    Their dyeing vats and looms;
Leave to the sons of Carthage
    The rudder and the oar;
Leave to the Greek his marble Nymphs
    And scrolls of wordy lore.

XXI

"Thine, Roman, is the pilum;
    Roman, the sword is thine,
The even trench, the bristling mound,
    The legion's ordered line;
And thine the wheels of triumph
    Which with their laureled train
Move slowly up the shouting streets
    To Jove's eternal fane.

XXII

"Beneath thy yoke the Volscian
    Shall vail his lofty brow;
Soft Capua's curled revelers
    Before thy chairs shall bow;
The Lucumoes of Arnus
    Shall quake thy rods [1] to see;
And the proud Samnite's heart of steel
    Shall yield to only thee.

[1] Rods of the lictors.

XXIII

"The Gaul shall come against thee
  From the land of snow and night;
Thou shalt give his fair-haired armies
  To the raven and the kite.

XXIV

"The Greek shall come against thee,
  The conqueror of the East.
Beside him stalks to battle
  The huge earth-shaking beast—
The beast on whom the castle
  With all its guards doth stand,
The beast who hath between his eyes
  The serpent for a hand.
First march the bold Epirotes,[1]
  Wedged close with shield and spear,
And the ranks of false Tarentum
  Are glittering in the rear.

XXV

"The ranks of false Tarentum
  Like hunted sheep shall fly;
In vain the bold Epirotes
  Shall round their standards die;
And Apennine's gray vultures
  Shall have a noble feast
On the fat and the eyes
  Of the huge earth-shaking beast.

XXVI

"Hurrah for the good weapons
  That keep the War-god's land!
Hurrah for Rome's stout pilum
  In a stout Roman hand!

[1] People from Epirus.

Hurrah for Rome's short broadsword,
  That through the thick array
Of leveled spears and serried shields
  Hews deep its gory way!

XXVII

"Hurrah for the great triumph
  That stretches many a mile!
Hurrah for the wan captives
  That pass in endless file!
Ho! bold Epirotes, whither
  Hath the Red King ta'en flight?
Ho! dogs of false Tarentum,
  Is not the gown washed white?

XXVIII

"Hurrah for the great triumph
  That stretches many a mile!
Hurrah for the rich dye of Tyre,
  And the fine web of Nile,
The helmets gay with plumage
  Torn from the pheasant's wings,
The belts set thick with starry gems
  That shone on Indian kings,
The urns of massy silver,
  The goblets rough with gold,
The many-colored tablets [1] bright
  With loves and wars of old,
The stone that breathes and struggles,
  The brass that seems to speak!—
Such cunning they who dwell on high
  Have given unto the Greek.

[1] Pictures.

XXIX

"Hurrah for Manius Curius,
  The bravest son of Rome,
Thrice in utmost need sent forth,
  Thrice drawn in triumph home!
Weave, weave, for Manius Curius
  The third embroidered gown;
Make ready the third lofty car,
  And twine the third green crown;
And yoke the steeds of Rosea
  With necks like a bended bow,
And deck the bull, Mevania's bull,
  The bull as white as snow.

XXX

"Blest and thrice blest the Roman
  Who sees Rome's brightest day,
Who sees that long victorious pomp
  Wind down the Sacred Way,
And through the bellowing Forum,
  And round the Suppliant's Grove,
Up to the everlasting gates
  Of Capitolian Jove.

XXXI

"Then where, o'er two bright havens
  The towers of Corinth frown;
Where the gigantic King of Day
  On his own Rhodes looks down;
Where soft Orontes murmurs
  Beneath the laurel shades;
Where Nile reflects the endless length
  Of dark-red colonnades;

> Where in the still deep water,
>   Sheltered from waves and blasts,
> Bristles the dusky forest
>   Of Byrsa's thousand masts; 280
> Where fur-clad hunters wander
>   Amidst the northern ice;
> Where through the sand of morning-land
>   The camel bears the spice;
> Where Atlas flings his shadow 285
>   Far o'er the western foam,
> Shall be great fear on all who hear
>   The mighty name of Rome."

IVRY

A SONG OF THE HUGUENOTS

Now glory to the Lord of Hosts, from whom all glories are!
And glory to our Sovereign Liege, King Henry of Navarre!
Now let there be the merry sound of music and of dance,
Through thy cornfields green, and sunny vines, oh pleasant land of France!
And thou, Rochelle,[1] our own Rochelle, proud city of the waters, 5
Again let rapture light the eyes of all thy mourning daughters.
As thou wert constant in our ills, be joyous in our joy,
For cold, and stiff, and still are they who wrought thy walls annoy.
Hurrah! Hurrah! a single field hath turned the chance of war,
Hurrah! Hurrah! for Ivry, and Henry of Navarre. 10

Oh! how our hearts were beating when, at the dawn of day,
We saw the army of the League drawn out in long array;
With all its priest-led citizens, and all its rebel peers,
And Appenzel's stout infantry, and Egmont's Flemish spears.
There rode the brood of false Lorraine, the curses of our land; 15
And dark Mayenne[2] was in the midst, a truncheon in his hand:
And, as we looked on them, we thought of Seine's enpurpled flood,
And good Coligni's hoary hair all dabbled with his blood;
And we cried unto the living God, who rules the fate of war,
To fight for His own holy name, and Henry of Navarre. 20

The King is come to marshal us, in all his armor drest,
And he has bound a snow-white plume upon his gallant crest.

---

[1] Headquarters of the Huguenots, situated on the Bay of Biscay.
[2] Guise's younger brother.

He looked upon his people, and a tear was in his eye;
He looked upon the traitors, and his glance was stern and high.
Right graciously he smiled on us, as rolled from wing to wing, 25
Down all our line, a deafening shout, "God save our Lord and King!"
"And if my standard-bearer fall, as fall full well he may,
For never saw I promise yet of such a bloody fray,
Press where ye see my white plume shine, amidst the ranks of war,
And be your oriflamme [1] to-day the helmet of Navarre." 30

Hurrah! the foes are moving. Hark to the mingled din
Of fife, and steed, and trump, and drum, and roaring culverin.
The fiery Duke [2] is pricking fast across Saint Andre's plain,
With all the hireling chivalry of Guelders [3] and Almayne.[4]
Now by the lips of those ye love, fair gentlemen of France, 35
Charge for the golden lilies,—upon them with the lance!
A thousand spurs are striking deep, a thousand spears in rest,
A thousand knights are pressing close behind the snow-white crest;
And in they burst, and on they rushed, while like a guiding star,
Amidst the thickest carnage blazed the helmet of Navarre. 40

Now, God be praised, the day is ours. Mayenne hath turned his rein.
D'Aumale [5] hath cried for quarter. The Flemish count is slain.
Their ranks are breaking like thin clouds before a Biscay gale;
The field is heaped with bleeding steeds, and flags, and cloven mail.
And then we thought on vengeance, and, all along our van, 45
"Remember St. Bartholomew!" was passed from man to man.
But out spake gentle Henry, "No Frenchman is my foe:

[1] Royal standard of France. [2] Mayenne.
[3] A province of Netherlands. [4] Germany. [5] First cousin of Guise.

Down, down with every foreigner, but let your brethren go."
Oh! was there ever such a knight in friendship or in war,
As our Sovereign Lord, King Henry, the soldier of Navarre? 50

Right well fought all the Frenchmen who fought for France to-day;
And many a lordly banner God gave them for a prey.
But we of the religion have borne us best in fight;
And the good Lord of Rosny has ta'en the cornet white.
Our own true Maximilian the cornet white hath ta'en, 55
The cornet white with crosses black, the flag of false Lorraine.
Up with it high; unfurl it wide; that all the host may know
How God hath humbled the proud house which wrought His church such woe.
Then on the ground, while trumpets sound the loudest point of war,
Fling the red shreds, a footcloth meet for Henry of Navarre. 60

Ho! maidens of Vienna; ho! matrons of Lucerne;
Weep, weep, and rend your hair for those who never shall return.
Ho! Philip, send, for charity, thy Mexican pistoles,
That Antwerp monks may sing a mass for thy poor spearmen's souls.
Ho! gallant nobles of the League, look that your arms be bright; 65
Ho! burghers of Saint Genevieve, keep watch and ward to-night.
For our God hath crushed the tyrant, our God hath raised the slave,
And mocked the counsel of the wise, and the valor of the brave.
Then glory to His holy name, from whom all glories are;
And glory to our Sovereign Lord, King Henry of Navarre. 70

THE BATTLE OF NASEBY

BY OBADIAH-BIND-THEIR-KINGS-IN-CHAINS-AND-THEIR-NOBLES-WITH-LINKS-OF-IRON, SERGEANT IN IRETON'S REGIMENT

Oh! wherefore come ye forth, in triumph from the North,
    With your hands, and your feet, and your raiment all red?
And wherefore doth your rout send forth a joyous shout?
    And whence be the grapes of the wine-press which ye tread?

Oh evil was the root, and bitter was the fruit,   5
    And crimson was the juice of the vintage that we trod;
For we trampled on the throng of the haughty and the strong,
    Who sate in the high places, and slew the saints of God.

It was about the noon of a glorious day of June,
    That we saw their banners dance, and their cuirasses shine,   10
And the Man of Blood [1] was there, with his long essenced hair,
    And Astley, and Sir Marmaduke, and Rupert of the Rhine.

Like a servant of the Lord, with his Bible and his sword,
    The General [2] rode along us to form us to the fight,
When a murmuring sound broke out, and swell'd into a shout,   15
    Among the godless horsemen upon the tyrant's right.[3]

And hark! like the roar of the billows on the shore,
    The cry of battle rises along their charging line!
For God! for the Cause! for the Church! for the Laws!
    For Charles, King of England, and Rupert of the Rhine!   20

[1] Charles I.   [2] Cromwell.   [3] See note on Rupert.

The furious German comes, with his clarions and his drums,
　His bravoes of Alsatia, and pages of Whitehall;
They are bursting on our flanks. Grasp your pikes, close your
　　　ranks;
　For Rupert never comes but to conquer or to fall.

They are here! They rush on! We are broken! We are gone! 25
　Our left is borne before them like stubble on the blast.
O Lord, put forth thy might! O Lord, defend the right!
　Stand back to back, in God's name, and fight it to the last.

Stout Skippon[1] hath a wound; the center hath given ground:
　Hark! hark!—What means the trampling of horsemen on
　　　our rear?   30
Whose banner do I see, boys? 'Tis he, thank God, 'tis he, boys,
　Bear up another minute: brave Oliver is here.

Their heads all stooping low, their points all in a row,
　Like a whirlwind on the trees, like a deluge on the dykes,
Our cuirassiers have burst on the ranks of the Accurst,   35
　And at a shock have scattered the forest of his pikes.

Fast, fast, the gallants ride, in some safe nook to hide
　Their coward heads, predestined to rot on Temple Bar;
And he—he turns, he flies:—shame on those cruel eyes
　That bore to look on torture, and dare not look on war.   40

Ho! comrades, scour the plain; and, ere ye strip the slain,
　First give another stab to make your search secure,
Then shake from sleeves and pockets their broad-pieces and
　　　lockets,
　The tokens of the wanton, the plunder of the poor.

[1] In command of the center division of Cromwell's troops.

Fools! your doublets shone with gold, and your hearts were
    gay and bold,   45
When you kissed your lily hands to your lemans [1] to-day;
And to-morrow shall the fox, from her chambers in the rocks,
    Lead forth her tawny cubs to howl above the prey.

Where be your tongues that late mocked at heaven and hell and
    fate,
And the fingers that once were so busy with your blades, 50
Your perfum'd satin clothes, your catches [2] and your oaths,
    Your stage-plays and your sonnets, your diamonds and your
    spades?

Down, down, for ever down with the miter and the crown,
    With the Belial [3] of the Court, and the Mammon of the
    Pope; [4]
There is woe in Oxford halls; there is wail in Durham's stalls; 55
    The Jesuit smites his bosom; the Bishop rends his cope.

And She [5] of the seven hills shall mourn her children's ills,
    And tremble when she thinks on the edge of England's sword;
And the Kings of earth in fear shall shudder when they hear
    What the hand of God hath wrought for the Houses [6] and
    the Word.[7]   60

[1] Lovers.
[2] Songs.
[3] Prince of devils in the Old Testament.
[4] The god of gold.
[5] Rome.
[6] Houses of Parliament.
[7] Word of God, *i.e.* the Bible.

THE ARMADA

A FRAGMENT

Attend, all ye who list to hear our noble England's praise;
I tell of the thrice famous deeds she wrought in ancient days,
When that great fleet invincible against her bore in vain
The richest spoils of Mexico, the stoutest hearts of Spain.

It was about the lovely close of a warm summer day, 5
There came a gallant merchant-ship full sail to Plymouth Bay;
Her crew hath seen Castile's [1] black fleet, beyond Auringy's isle,[2]
At earliest twilight, on the waves lie heaving many a mile.
At sunrise she escaped their van, by God's especial grace;
And the tall Pinta, till the noon, had held her close in chase. 10
Forthwith a guard at every gun was placed along the wall;
The beacon blazed upon the roof of Edgecumbe's [3] lofty hall;
Many a light fishing-bark put out to pry along the coast,
And with loose rein and bloody spur rode inland many a post.
With his white hair unbonneted, the stout old sheriff comes; 15
Behind him march the halberdiers; before him sound the drums;
His yeomen round the market cross make clear an ample space;
For there behooves him to set up the standard of Her Grace.[4]
And haughtily the trumpets peal, and gaily dance the bells,
As slow upon the laboring wind the royal blazon swells. 20
Look how the Lion of the sea lifts up his ancient crown,
And underneath his deadly paw treads the gay lilies down!
So stalked he when he turned to flight, on that famed Picard field,
Bohemia's plume, and Genoa's bow, and Cæsar's eagle shield.

[1] Spain's.
[2] Alderney, situated in the English Channel.
[3] A headland on Plymouth Sound.
[4] Queen Elizabeth.

So glared he when at Agincourt in wrath he turned to bay, 25
And crushed and torn beneath his claws the princely hunters lay.
Ho! strike the flagstaff deep, Sir Knight; ho! scatter flowers, fair maids;
Ho! gunners, fire a loud salute; ho! gallants, draw your blades;
Thou sun, shine on her joyously; ye breezes, waft her wide;
Our glorious SEMPER EADEM, the banner of our pride. 30
The freshening breeze of eve unfurled that banner's massy fold;
The parting gleam of sunshine kissed that haughty scroll of gold;
Night sank upon the dusky beach, and on the purple sea,
Such night in England ne'er had been, nor ne'er again shall be.
From Eddystone to Berwick bounds, from Lynn to Milford Bay, 35
That time of slumber was as bright and busy as the day;
For swift to east and swift to west the ghastly war-flame spread,
High on St. Michael's Mount [1] it shone; it shone on Beachy Head.[2]
Far on the deep the Spaniard saw, along each southern shire,
Cape beyond cape, in endless range, those twinkling points of fire. 40
The fisher left his skiff to rock on Tamar's glittering waves;
The rugged miners poured to war from Mendip's sunless caves;
O'er Longleat's towers, o'er Cranbourne's oaks, the fiery herald flew:
He roused the shepherds of Stonehenge, the rangers of Beaulieu.
Right sharp and quick the bells all night rang out from Bristol town, 45
And ere the day three hundred horse had met on Clifton down;
The sentinel on Whitehall [3] gate looked forth into the night,

---

[1] A rock off the southwestern coast of England.
[2] A headland in Sussex, southeastern England.
[3] Then the royal residence in London.

And saw o'erhanging Richmond Hill [1] the streak of blood-red light.
Then bugle's note and cannon's roar the deathlike silence broke,
And with one start, and with one cry, the royal city woke.   50
At once on all her stately gates arose the answering fires;
At once the wild alarum clashed from all her reeling spires;
From all the batteries of the Tower [2] pealed loud the voice of fear;
And all the thousand masts of Thames sent back a louder cheer;
And from the furthest wards was heard the rush of hurrying feet,   55
And the broad streams of pikes and flags rushed down each roaring street;
And broader still became the blaze, and louder still the din,
As fast from every village round the horse came spurring in;
And eastward straight from wild Blackheath [3] the warlike errand went,
And roused in many an ancient hall the gallant squires of Kent.
Southward from Surrey's pleasant hills flew those bright couriers forth;   61
High on bleak Hampstead's [4] swarthy moor they started for the north;
And on, and on, without a pause, untired they bounded still;
All night from tower to tower they sprang; they sprang from hill to hill:
Till the proud peak unfurled the flag o'er Darwin's rocky dales,   65
Till like volcanoes flared to heaven the stormy hills of Wales,
Till twelve fair counties saw the blaze on Malvern's lonely height,
Till streamed in crimson on the wind the Wrekin's crest of light,
Till broad and fierce the star came forth on Ely's stately fane,

---

[1] A part of London, to the westward.
[2] The ancient palace-citadel of London.
[3] An open common.
[4] Now a part of London.

And tower and hamlet rose in arms o'er all the boundless
   plain; 70
Till Belvoir's [1] lordly terraces the sign to Lincoln sent,
And Lincoln sped the message on o'er the wide vale of Trent;
Till Skiddaw [2] saw the fire that burned on Gaunt's embattled
   pile,
And the red glare on Skiddaw roused the burghers of Carlisle.

*   *   *   *   *   *   *   *   *   *

[1] Seat of the Duke of Rutland, in Leicestershire.
[2] A mountain in Cumberland, northeastern England.

NOTES

METER OF THE POEMS. Macaulay in a very interesting letter to his friend Ellis (see Trevelyan, Vol. II, p. 106) speaks of the remarkable coincidence by which the meter chosen for *Horatius* should be, without intention, so very similar to that probably used by the old Roman ballad writers. This was the Saturnian meter, technically explained by Macaulay as acatalectic iambic dimeter followed by three trochees, which means a line not cut off (catalectic) at the end, i. e. not lacking a syllable, consisting of four iambic (short, long) feet, and three trochaic (long, short) feet. It is called a "dimeter" (two measure) line because iambi are measured in pairs. The line may be represented thus

$$\smile - | \smile - | \smile - | \smile - \| - \smile | - \smile | - \smile |$$

Macaulay exemplifies it in English by the nursery rime

> The queen was in her parlor
> Eating bread and honey.

This quotation shows why *Horatius*, *Regillus*, and *Capys* have what is one line written as two half lines, whereas in *Virginia* the half lines are discarded.

The occasional change in the stanza form is due to a desire to make it more suitable to the thought. It occurs when the action is rapid or at points of intense interest.

There is often found what is called line rime, that is the word in the middle of the line rimes with the one at the end. Though not invariably yet often it is found toward the end of a stanza and seems to serve the duty of preparing for and indicating the approach of the end. This is similar to the use of a rime toward the end of a scene in Shakespeare's non-riming plays, such as *Macbeth*.

HORATIUS

CCCLX. The Romans counted the years from the founding of the city (*ab urbe condita*, abbreviated to A. U. C.) as we count them from the birth of Christ. This year equals 394 B. C.

1. **Lars Porsena** (Pŏr'se-na). A Roman legendary king of Etruria.—**Clusium.** A city of Etruria, about 80 miles north of Rome.

2. **Nine Gods.** The Etruscans had nine gods. Their mythology differed from the Roman.

3. **house of Tarquin.** That is, the family of the Tarquins.

4. **suffer wrong.** These former kings of Rome had been banished on account of the crime of Sextus, who outraged Lucretia. The story runs that a bet was made in the camp among some young men as to the occupation of their wives. On their riding home, Lucretia was found at work while the other women were found amusing themselves. Sextus became inflamed by her beauty and later committed the deed. Lucretia killed herself.

25. **Apennine.** Mountains north of Etruria.

26. **lordly Volaterræ.** In Etruria. "Lordly" because it stands on a hill 1700 feet high.

30. **Populonia.** A coast city of Etruria, opposite Sardinia.

34. **Pisæ.** A commercial city on the Arno.

36. **Massilia.** Marseilles.—**triremes.** Boats or galleys rowed by slaves seated in three tiers.

37. **fair-haired slaves.** Prisoners of war became slaves. These were Gauls.

38. **Clanis.** A river flowing into the Tiber.

40. **Cortona.** A city near Lake Trasimenus, on a lofty hill.

43. **Auser's rill.** In northwest Etruria.

45. **Ciminian hill.** A mountain range northwest of Rome.

46. **Clitumnus.** A river of Umbria.

49. **Volsinian mere.** A lake in southern Etruria.

58. **Arretium.** A town in northwest Etruria.

60. **Umbro.** A large river in Etruria.

61. **plunge the struggling sheep.** Washing before shearing.

NOTES

62. Luna. A town in the extreme northwest of Etruria.

64. feet of laughing girls. Grapes were pressed by the bare feet.

65. sires have marched to Rome. The work of the men who had gone to war had to be done by those left: the old men, the boys, and the women.

71. turned the verses o'er. Before any undertaking ancient people consulted the wise men who referred to their sacred books.

72. Traced from the right. Etruscans wrote from the right to the left as is done in Hebrew.

75. glad. Because they foresaw victory.

80. Nurscia's altars. Nurscia was the Etruscan goddess of Fate, worshiped at Volsinii.

81. golden shields. Legend says one shield fell from heaven; others were made like it. It was believed that Rome would endure as long as they were kept in the city.

86. Sutrium. A city twenty-nine miles northwest of Rome.

96. Mamilius. Son-in-law of Tarquin, of Tusculum in Latium.

100. champaign. Flat, open country. Rome is surrounded by such a formation.

115. skins of wine. In ancient times skins of animals were used instead of bottles or barrels.

122. rock Tarpeian. The Capitoline Hill in Rome. In the Sabine War, Tarpeia, the daughter of the keeper, promised to open its gates to the enemy if they gave her what they wore on their left arms, *i. e.* their gold ornaments. But when they entered they crushed her with their heavy shields from their left arms.

126. Fathers of the City. The old men composing the Senate.

131. Tuscan. Modern form of "Etruscan," the adjective from Etruria.

133. Crustumerium. In Latium, a few miles northeast of Rome.

134. Verbenna. An Etruscan leader. The name was invented by Macaulay. The word is the subject of "hath wasted."—**Ostia.** Seaport at the mouth of the Tiber.

136. Astur. A name also invented by the author.—**Janiculum.** A hill on the west bank of the Tiber opposite Rome.

138. I wis. A spurious word arising from the Middle English adverb *iwis* (German, *gewis*), meaning "certainly." *I wis* is used as if it were the pres. ind., 1st per. sing. of a verb *wis* which does not exist. The real verb is *wit*, meaning "know." Pres. ind., 1st per. *wot*. The only common use of this verb is the infinitive *to wit*.

144. girded. Bound as with a cord or sash.—**gowns.** The chief article of a male Roman's dress was the *toga*, a long, flowing, loose over-garment something like a gown.

145. wall. Rome was a walled town.

147. River-Gate. The wall had several gates. This one was on the riverside.

151. The bridge. Called the *Pons Sublicius*, bridge on piles, connecting with the hill of Janiculum.

177. twelve. The number in the Etruscan confederacy.

180. Umbrian. Umbria was a province east of Etruria.

181. Gaul. Inhabitant of Gallia, ancient name of what is now chiefly France. "Terror," because the Etruscans had defeated both of them in war.

185. Lucumo. Etruscan princes and priests.

186. Cilnius. A powerful Etruscan noble.

188. fourfold. Made of four layers of oxhide.

190. Tolumnius. Another Etruscan leader.

192. Thrasymene. Lake Trasimenus in eastern Etruria.

200. deed of shame. See note on **suffer wrong**, l. 4.

213. van. Vanguard; advance part of an army.

217. Horatius. Surnamed *Cocles*, "the one-eyed." He belonged to the tribe of the Luceres, one of the three forming the patrician or upper section of Roman society.

218. The Captain of the Gate. In charge of troops there.

223. ashes of his fathers. The Romans burned their dead and preserved the ashes in urns. See Johnston's *Private Life of the Romans*, p. 314.

229. holy maidens. Vesta was the goddess of the hearth. Before the shrine a fire was always kept burning by six virgin priestesses.

236. hold . . . in play. Keep occupied.

242. Ramnian. The Ramnes formed the second of the patrician tribes.

246. Titian. The Tities formed the third tribe. Thus as Macaulay pointed out in his introductory note (see p. 25), each of the three tribes was represented.

267. Tribunes. Civil representatives of the commons or plebeians.—**the high.** The patricians.

268. the low. The plebeians.

278. crow. An instrument shaped like the beak of a crow, for tearing apart.

301. Aunus, etc. Some of these names are invented, others are common. Of course all these details are made up.—**Tifernum.** A town in Umbria.

304. Sicken. Because of the hard life.—**Ilva's mines.** The iron mines on the island of Ilva (modern Elba), off the coast of Etruria.

309. Nequinum. A town in Umbria on a lofty rock, called by the Romans *Narnia.*—**lowers.** Frowns, because seeming to look down threateningly.

310. Nar. A river in Umbria flowing into the Tiber.

319. Falerii. An important town of south Etruria.

321. Urgo. An island in the Tyrrhenian Sea.

323. Volsinium. An Etruscan town on a high rock. Properly *Volsinii.*

326. Cosa. An Etrurian seaport.—**fen.** Lowland partially covered by water, producing coarse growths, as reeds.

328. Albinia. An Etruscan river.

337. Campania. A province southeast of Rome.

346. for a space. For a time.

360. she-wolf's litter. According to the legend Romulus and Remus, who had been exposed on the banks of the Tiber by the order of Amulius, were found and nursed by a she-wolf as if they belonged to her own litter. Growing up they founded Rome. Hence the Romans, their descendants, could be called the "she-wolf's litter."

384. Alvernus. Near the source of the Tiber.

388. augurs. The priests who foretold the future.

417. Was none. There was none.

465. turret-tops. The tops of the towers on the walls.

467. unbroken. Not accustomed to harness.

470. mane. Referring to the foam.

471. curb. Continuing the figure, the broken bridge is called the curb or bit in the mouth.

474. Battlement. The parts for defense.

488. Palatinus. One of the hills of Rome.

508. Tuscany. The modern name of Etruria.

525. Bore bravely up his chin. To this line the author placed as a footnote the following quotations:

> "Our ladye bare upp her chinne."
> *Ballad of Childe Waters.*

> "Never heavier man and horse
> Stemmed a midnight torrent's force;
>
> . . . .
>
> Yet, through good heart and our Lady's grace,
> At length he gained the landing place."
> *Lay of the Last Minstrel,* I.

They were given because of the similarity to the text.

543. public right. Belonging to the state.

546. molten image. A figure made from melted metal.

549. I. The citizen narrating the story. See Macaulay's Introduction.

550. Comitium. Part of the Roman *forum* or public market place.

561. charge . . . home. Fight effectively.—**Volscian.** People living in the southern part of Latium. At the supposed date of this poem the Romans had just subdued them.

562. Juno. Queen of the gods.

572. Algidus. A mountain in Latium, about twelve miles from Rome.

577. spit. A device for roasting over an open fire.

584. shuttle. The mother is weaving cloth. The shuttle carries the thread back and forth through the upright threads.

585. loom. Machine for weaving. It holds the upright threads.

The Action after the Incident of the Bridge

After the bridge fell Lars Porsena with his army laid siege to the city. The food supply running short, the people were threatened with famine. At this crisis Mucius, a noble Roman, secretly entered the camp of Porsena to kill him in the hope that the army would retire if its leader were slain. But by mistake he slew another, and being captured was brought before the general for sentence. To show his fearlessness he let the flames on an altar consume his right hand. His boldness and endurance so aroused the admiration of Porsena that he set him free. In gratitude Mucius revealed a determined plot to kill the Etruscan. Alarmed for his safety Porsena made peace with the Romans who gave him certain hostages. Among these was a girl named Cloelia, who, escaping, swam the Tiber to Rome. But the Romans kept their faith, and though they admired Cloelia's pluck, returned her to Porsena. Thereupon, filled with admiration for the Romans' faith, he released Cloelia and other hostages whom she selected. Porsena then returned to Clusium.

THE BATTLE OF THE LAKE REGILLUS

Regillus. A small body of water near Rome. It no longer exists.—**Castor and Pollux.** Twin gods noted for their skill with horses.—**Ides.** The 15th.—**Quintilis.** The old fifth month, later named July.—**The year of the city CCCCLI.** B. C. 303.

2. **lictors.** Officers who attended Roman magistrates to enforce respect. They carried the *fasces* or rods bound in a bundle from the middle of which an ax protruded.

3. **Knights.** The equestrian order of citizens. At first they were merely cavalry, but later a class of society.

7. **Castor.** A statue of the god.

8. **Mars.** A statue of the god.—**without the wall.** Outside of the fortifications of the city.

10. **crowned.** The olive crown of the knights at their imperial review typified gifts of peace that, in a barbarous age, could be secured by victory alone.

13. **Yellow River.** The Tiber. See *Horatius*, l. 98.

14. **Sacred Hill.** A mountain near Rome to which the people once retired when in distress. By this secession they gained the election of representatives called Tribunes.

17. **Martian Kalends.** March first.

18. **December's Nones.** December fifth.
20. **whitest.** Lucky days were marked with chalk or a white stone.
24. **Came.** Came to the scene of the battle.
25. **Parthenius.** A mountain in southern Greece.
27. **Cirrha.** A town north of the mountain.
31. **Lacedæmon.** The beginning of their route. The old name for Sparta in Greece.
32. **two kings.** Sparta had two kings as Rome had two consuls.
34. **Porcian height.** A hill near Tusculum.
42. **Corne.** A hill remarkable for the size of its trees.
63. **Thirty Cities.** A league of the thirty cities of Latium.
69. **hoof mark.** The legend relates that one of the divine steeds of the gods made an impress of his hoof on the margin of Lake Regillus.
70. **into the flint.** The volcanic rock in the soil.
77. **Great Twin Brethren.** See Introduction, p. 49.
83. **Aulus.** Aulus Posthumius (properly spelled "Postumius").
84. **race.** A group of families or *gens*.
86. **Gabii.** One of the towns of the Latin league.
105. **eyrie.** Old spelling of "aerie," nest of an eagle.
106. **carrion kite.** The kite is a kind of hawk.
119. **Conscript Fathers.** Translation of *patres conscripti*, shortened form of *patres et conscripti*, a term applied to the Senators, who were originally patricians and called *patres*. Later when plebeians were added to the Senate they were *conscripti*, "added to the roll." Hence the term.
123. **Dictator.** An officer with absolute authority, appointed in times of great danger for six months by a consul at the order of the Senate.
125. **Camerium.** A town in Latium.
131. **Master of the Knights.** An assistant appointed by the Dictator.
132. **axes.** Lictors who bore axes. See note on lictors, l. 2.
165. **Setia.** A town of Latium above the Pontine marshes.
166. **Norba.** Another town of Latium.
169. **Witch's Fortress.** Circeii, on a promontory in Latium, where the enchantress Circe is supposed to have dwelt.

NOTES

172. **Aricia.** A town in Latium, near which is a lake.

174. **ghastly priest.** In Aricia was a famous temple of Diana whose priest was a fugitive slave. According to custom he had obtained his position by killing his predecessor and in like manner would in turn be killed.

177. **Ufens.** A muddy, sluggish stream of Latium.

183. **Cora.** An ancient city of Latium, notable for remains of huge stone walls.

185. **Laurentian.** Marshes near Laurentum, a seacoast city and the ancient capital of Latium.

187. **Anio.** A river flowing into the Tiber above Rome, after a fine waterfall.

190. **Velitræ.** An ancient town of Latium, east of Rome.

201. **land of sunrise.** The East.

203. **Carthage.** The chief Phœnician city in the north of Africa. It carried on an extensive commerce.

205. **Lavinium.** A town of Latium.

207. **marsh.** Pontine marshes near Rome.

217. **A woman.** A vision of Lucretia whom he had outraged and who killed herself.

219. **watches.** The Romans divided the night into periods according to the tours of duty of sentinels.

221. **distaff.** A primitive instrument for spinning.

233. **Tibur.** A famous ancient town, the modern Tivoli, twenty miles from Rome.—**Pedum.** A town of Latium, ten miles from Rome.

235. **Ferentinum.** A town in Latium.

236. **pool.** The town was on a small lake.

237. **succors.** Allies from the Volscians, a people of Latium.

240. **king.** Tarquinius Superbus. See p. 24.

241. **Soracte.** A mountain in southern Etruria, famous in literature.

249. **Titus.** The youngest son of Tarquinius Superbus.

250. **Apulian.** Apulia, a province in southeast Italy, well adapted to the raising of horses.

263. **Pomptine.** The vapor that rises from the Pontine Marshes, *Pomptinae Paludes*, which are in Latium between the coast and

the Volscian Mountains, seven miles in breadth and thirty-one miles in length. Macaulay uses " Pomptine," which is nearer the Latin.

278. Digentian rock. A small hill above the junction of the River Digentia with the Anio.

280. Bandusia's flock. Flock from the Fountain of Bandusia in Apulia, originally thought to be in the country of the Sabines.

283. Auster. The name of his horse. It is also the name of the south wind.

287. crown. Crowns were granted for distinctive service in war.

288. Fidenæ. A town of Latium captured by the Romans.

294. Calabrian brake. A thicket in Calabria, the heel of Italy.

325. clients. Persons in Rome who put themselves under the protection of another, usually a patrician, called a patron.

362. Velian hill. In Rome, between the Palatine and Esquiline hills.

372. A span. The distance between the tip of the thumb and the tip of the little finger when the hand is spread.

383. yeomen. Members of his bodyguard.

399. play the men. Act as men should act.

416. Consular. Adjective used as a noun. Man of consular rank, one who has been a consul.

441. southward battle. The division of troops at the south.

480. Aufidus. A river of southeast Italy in Apulia.—**Po.** A river of northern Italy.

557. The furies. Goddesses, called "The Eumenides," who as avengers of crime plagued the criminal.

568. Capuan. Capua was a city of Campania noted for luxury.

582. Auster's band. Girth round the horse to hold the saddle cloth.

603. Samothracia. An island in the Ægean Sea.

604. Cyrene. A celebrated city in Libya, Africa.

605. Tarentum. A Greek town in Calabria, noted for luxury.

607. Syracuse. A powerful Greek city of Sicily, noted for extensive shipping.

609. Eurotas. A river of Greece near Sparta, their home.

619. Ardea. A town of Latium, here used in the sense of "the men of Ardea." So "the men of Cora," l. **620.**

631. swell. A gradual increase, followed by a decrease of sound.

NOTES

646. Celtic plain. That part of northern Italy which the Gauls, who were Celts, occupied when they crossed the Alps. It is generally called Gallia Cisalpina.

648. Adrian main. The expanse of the Adriatic Sea.

649. Sire Quirinus. A name given to Romulus after he was carried away by Mars to heaven.

660. Lanuvium fled. That is, the men of the town of Lanuvium, in Latium.

661. Nomentum. A town of Latium.

673. Arpinum. A town of Latium, famous as the birthplace of Cicero.

676. Anxur. A town near the Pontine Marshes.

695. Twelve. The men who took care of the shields.

696. Golden Shield. See *Horatius*, note on l. 81.

697. High Pontiff. The *Pontifex Maximus*, chief priest.

699. Etruria's colleges. "College" means a gathering. Etruria instructed Rome in many things.

716. pricking. Hurrying by the use of the spur.

721. Asylum. Romulus set aside a part of the city as a refuge for those fleeing from other places.

722. seven. Rome was situated on seven hills.

724. heaven. See *Horatius*, note on l. 81.

742. laurel boughs. Emblems of victory.

745. nigh to Vesta. That is, to her temple.

760. Dorians. These two gods had their home in Sparta whose inhabitants belonged to the Dorian branch of the Greeks.

768. sails. Castor and Pollux later were made into a constellation of two stars which has been confounded with the electrical display seen sometimes on ships at sea.

781. Unto the Great Twin Brethren. That is, to their temple.

VIRGINIA

5. running wine. In Euripides's *Bacchæ* characters are represented as striking the ground from which fountains of wine issued. Macaulay was very fond of this play.

6. snaky tresses. See the myth of the Furies and that of Medusa in a classical dictionary.—**swine.** See the myth of Circe.

10. wicked Ten. Decemvirs. See Macaulay's Introduction, p. 77.

12. Appius Claudius. See Introduction, p. 77.

14. axes. Lictors. See *Regillus*, note on l. 2.

20. client. See *Regillus*, note on l. 325.

23. lying Greeks. The Romans despised the Greeks.

24. Licinius. See Introduction, p. 76.

31. tablets. Smooth plates of wood or ivory, covered with a thin layer of wax, protected by raised edges, hinged together by wire, and written upon with a pointed instrument of iron called a *stylus*.

35. Sacred Street. The *Via Sacra*, a celebrated street of Rome, so called probably because upon it were some of the greatest sanctuaries.

38. Lucrece. See *Horatius*, note on l. 4.—**combing the fleece.** Disentangling the fleece of sheep preparatory to spinning.

45. Alban mountains. Fifteen miles from Rome, in Latium.

70. caitiff. One who is both wicked and mean.

74. sickness. A great plague raged in Rome in B. C. 463.

75. month of wail and fright. September is a very unhealthy month in Rome.

76. augurs. An augur foretold the future by interpreting such signs as the flight of birds.—**borne forth.** Carried out dead from their houses.

87. Icilius. An imaginary character who took the opportunity to stir up the people to revolt.

89. column. The *pila Horatia* on which were displayed the spoils of the fight between the Curatii, the champions of the Albans, and the Horatii, those of the Romans.

95. Servius. Servius Tullius, an early king who gave the people a constitution.

97. false sons. In the first attempt of Tarquin to regain his throne the conspirators included two sons of the Consul, Lucius Junius Brutus, who had the lictor put them to death like the others. On Tarquin's attempts see page 24.

98. Scævola. In the siege of Rome, during Tarquin's third attempt, Mucius, a Roman noble, went to Porsena's camp to kill him, but was captured. To show his contempt for any punishment, he calmly let his right hand burn in a fire. Henceforth he was called *Scævola*, "left-handed."

99. **fox-earth.** Fox's hole standing for the fox himself, referring to the Decemvirs. Shall they awe the people who overthrew the kings (lion's den)?

101. **the Senate's will.** Since the Senate was mostly composed of patricians, the successful efforts of the people to obtain their rights from time to time may be thought of as curbing the will of the former.

102. **Sacred Hill.** In one of their attempts, B. C. 494, to gain their rights, the plebeians marched away to a hill beyond the Anio. After terms were made, the hill was called the Sacred Hill or Mount.

104. **Marcian fury.** During a famine some ships laden with corn came from Syracuse. Caius Marcius Coriolanus thereupon proposed that none be distributed till the plebeians had consented to give up their tribunes. The tribunes impeached him before the assembly of the tribes and he had to flee.—**Fabian pride.** The Fabian *gens*, or group of families, usurped the consulship for ten years. After a while they were all compelled to leave Rome.

105. **Quinctius.** Cæso, son of Lucius Quinctius, who often drove the tribunes from the forum and put the plebeians to flight. He fled after being brought to trial.

106. **Claudius.** Probably this refers to one of the family whose soldiers rebelled against him.

108. **blighted in a day.** When the Decemvirs were elected in B. C. 451, to draw up a code of laws, they were given power to act as supreme magistrates until the new code came into force, all other magistrates being suspended, and the plebeians giving up their tribunes. The effort to secure these tribunes originally had been the work of years. Further, the Decemvirs ruled arbitrarily; hence all the plebeians' successfully established rights were swept away.

111. **No crier.** The herald, who called the men to the voting.

115. **holy fillets.** Ceremonial headdress of the priests, who were patricians.—**purple gown.** Insignia of a Senator.

116. **curule chair.** The chair of state used by the consuls.—**the car.** The chariot used in triumphal processions by generals, who

were chiefly patricians.—**laurel crown.** The emblem of victory worn by the generals.

117. **press.** Cause us to serve.—**cohorts.** A cohort was the tenth part of a legion or body of soldiers.

120. **usance.** Interest for the use of money.

122. **dens of torment.** Prisons where debtors who could not pay were placed.

123. **dog-star heat.** The period when the Dog Star, Sirius, was visible.

124. **holes.** Stocks for punishment by confining the feet.

127. **Shades.** The spirits of the dead who inhabited Hades, a place considered to exist below the earth.

130. **High Pontiffs.** Chief Priests.—**Alban Kings.** Kings of Alba Longa, a city more ancient than Rome and the old capital of Latium.

133. **Corinthian mirrors.** Made in Corinth of polished metal.

134. **Capuan.** See *Regillus*, note on l. 568.

157. **civic crown.** *Corona civica*, made of oak leaves. It was given to a soldier for saving the life of a citizen.

162. **upon his urn.** The receptacle of a person's ashes after cremation.

167. **he.** Appius Claudius.

182. **Volscians.** A people inhabiting the coast of Latium with whom the Romans had had much trouble.

192. **judgment seat.** The official place where Appius Claudius was sitting.

193. **dwellers in the nether gloom.** Gods of the lower regions with their ministers of vengeance, the Furies.

213. **cypress crown.** The cypress was a death emblem in Rome.

224. **sheaf of twigs.** The fasces. See *Regillus*, note on l. 2.

228. **Pincian Hill.** In the northern part of the city.—**the Latin Gate.** The gate on the *Via Latina* leading to Tusculum.

244. **potsherds.** Broken pieces of earthenware.

249. **Caius.** Coriolanus. See note on l. 104.

251. **Furius.** Marcus Furius Camillus who captured Veii in southern Etruria, a town with which Rome had been at war for centuries. He is also said to have driven away the Gauls under Brennus.

NOTES

255. within the city towers. That is, inside of the city.

259. litter. Litter is used as the offspring of a dog, so here it is contemptuous.

266. necks. The chair was carried on their shoulders.

276. Adriatic. It is noted for its storms.

277. sea-marks. Lights on the west coast of the "heel" of Italy.

278. Thunder Cape. Acroceraunia in Epirus, western Greece, nearly opposite the "heel" of Italy. The name is from the Greek and means derivatively "the thunder-smitten peaks."

EVENTS AFTER THE DEATH OF VIRGINIA

After he had killed his daughter Virginius hurried to the army which took up his cause. The troops marched to the city and encamped on the Aventine where they were joined by the other army. All the soldiers then took station on the Sacred Mount, the scene of the first Plebeian Secession. The situation was so acute that the Decemvirs were compelled to resign. The Patricians sent Valerius and Horatius, men of known moderation, as envoys to treat with the army. An agreement was entered upon by which the tribunes were restored. As soon as they assumed office these officials proceeded against the Decemvirs. Appius Claudius and another were put into prison where they committed suicide and the rest went into exile.

THE PROPHECY OF CAPYS

Dentatus. See Introduction, p. 90.

1. Amulius. See Introduction, p. 90. The entire legend is as follows: Æneas after the fall of Troy came to Italy where he was well received by King Latinus who gave him his daughter Lavinia in marriage. Æneas built a town called Lavinium after his wife. At his death his son Ascanius became king. He built a new city on Mt. Albanus called Alba Longa. His descendants ruled in regular order till after the death of Procas. This king left two sons Numitor and Amulius. The latter, the younger, usurped the throne and to make his position secure killed Numitor's son and made his daughter, Rhea Silvia, a vestal virgin in order that she might have no children. But she bore to the god Mars twins, Romulus and Remus. Then the doom was pronounced according to law that the mother be buried alive and the children thrown into the Tiber, then in flood. But the basket containing the children came to the shore, where they were suckled by a she-wolf. Later they were found by a shepherd who brought them up. The twins became great hunters and collected a band of devoted young men. Discovering their birth they marched to Alba with their followers, killed Amulius, and restored Numitor to the throne. Macaulay gives the priest a name and has the brothers kill him too. Later they left Alba to found a city on one of the hills of the Tiber. This city was Rome, named from Romulus.

23. **the dead.** The twins. This is the day on which they have come back and restored their grandfather to the throne.

58. **horsehair.** The helmet had a plume of horsehair.

71. **holy fillets.** See *Virginia*, note on l. 115.

99. **foster child.** A child nursed or brought up by one not its own mother.

104. **The bison in the stall.** He likens Romulus to the eagle and to the bison implying that he has as much place there as an eagle in a hencoop or a bison in the stall of a stable.

110. **Tartessian.** Adjective from Tartessus, Latin name of Tarshish, a district of southern Spain.

112. **Libyan brine.** That part of the Mediterranean Sea along the coast of Libya, Africa.

113. **amber.** For cups ornamented with amber.

115. **steep thy locks.** " Cause thy hair to be permeated with perfume." Arabia was noted for its perfumes.

116. **Sidon tinge.** Sidon in Phœnicia was noted for dyes. " These will not color thy gown."

117. **myrrh.** A gum used for perfume.

118. **Rich table.** Luxurious food.

130. **Vesta.** See *Horatius*, note on l. 229.

133. **ox.** In Italy the ox was used for pulling the plow.

149. **Pomona.** A nymph who was the goddess of fruit trees.

150. **Liber.** Bacchus, the god of wine.

151. **Pales.** The goddess of sheepfolds.

169. **Campanian.** The Campanians were noted for their effeminacy and luxury.

171. Tyre. A Phœnician city famous for dyes and woven garments.

173. Carthage. A city on the northern coast of Africa. It was powerful on the sea and a great rival of Rome.

175. marble Nymphs. Sculpture.

176. wordy lore. Literature.

177. pilum. A heavy wooden javelin with a long iron point.

179. bristling mound. The fortifications of a Roman camp consisted mainly of a trench or ditch, the earth from which was piled up at its edge to make a mound or wall, faced partly with sod and partly with bundles of sticks.

180. legion. A body of soldiers like a regiment.

181. wheels of triumph. Successful generals were given a triumph, a procession in which the general wearing a wreath of bay, rode in a car accompanied by soldiers, captives, and the spoils of war.

182. laureled train. The soldiers in the triumph wore laurel.

184. fane. The temple where the triumphs ended with a sacrifice to Jupiter.

185. yoke. The soldiers of a conquered army, in token of submission and degradation, were compelled to pass "under the yoke," a device consisting of three spears, two planted in the ground and the third fastened across them.—**Volscian.** See *Horatius*, note on l. 561. There were many contests between the Romans and Volscians.

186. vail. Bow in token of submission.

187. revelers. See l. 169. They paid much attention to personal adornment.

188. chairs. Curule chairs. See *Virginia*, note on l. 116.

189. Lucumoes. See *Horatius*, note on l. 185.—**Arnus.** A river in northern Etruria.

191. Samnite. Inhabitants of Samnium, a region east of Latium.

194. land of snow and night. The north is so considered by those living in the south.

197. The Greek. In the person of Pyrrhus, king of Epirus.

198. The conqueror. Under Alexander the Greeks subdued the East.

200. beast. The elephant.

201. castle. On the backs of the elephants were fortlike structures filled with soldiers.

207. **false Tarentum.** See Introduction, p. 90.

223. **shields.** This line refers to the Greek military formation known as the phalanx, in which the soldiers, drawn up in several ranks, so held their spears that the points of all were presented to the enemy, while their large shields afforded themselves protection.

230. **Red King.** Pyrrhus means "red" in Greek.

232. **washed white.** See Introduction, p. 90.

236. **web of Nile.** Egypt was famous for its woven stuffs.

240. **Indian kings.** The Greeks had warred with the natives of India.

245. **stone that breathes and struggles.** Lifelike statues.

246. **brass that seems to speak.** Bronze statues.

249. **Curius.** See Title, p. 92.

252. **Thrice . . . home.** He won three great victories.

254. **embroidered gown.** The gown, car, and crown belonged to the triumph.

257. **Rosea.** A valley near Reate.

259. **Mevania.** A town in Umbria.

265. **bellowing Forum.** The people were shouting in the Forum.

266. **Suppliant's Grove.** The place where Romulus made the asylum. See *Regillus*, note on l. 721.

268. **Capitolian Jove.** Temple of Jove on the Capitoline Hill.

269. **bright havens.** Corinth had two harbors.

271. **King of Day.** The Colossus of Rhodes, a gigantic statue bestriding the entrance to the port.

273. **Orontes.** A river in Syria.

280. **Byrsa.** The citadel of Carthage.

283. **sand of morning-land.** Deserts of the east.

285. **Atlas.** Mountains in northern Africa.

IVRY

Ivry. A small place in Normandy. Here in 1590 the battle of the same name was fought between the Catholic League, under the Duke of Mayenne, and the Huguenots, under King Henry of Navarre. The latter was the rightful successor to the throne of France; but,

NOTES

chiefly because of his religion, the League disputed his succession. Henry, at the head of the Protestant (Huguenot) forces, vindicated his right by defeating the allies at Ivry.

14. Appenzel. A canton in Switzerland.—**Egmont's Flemish spears.** Flanders at this time was under Spanish rule, hence in the League. Egmont was leading the Flemish division.

15. Lorraine. A French province under the rulership of the Duke of Guise, one of the founders of the League.

18. Coligni. A leader of the Huguenots, said to be the first one murdered in the massacre of St. Bartholomew.

46. St. Bartholomew. The massacre of the French Protestants, on St. Bartholomew's eve and day (August 23-24), 1572. Some 25,000 were slain.

54. Lord of Rosny. Maximilian. Afterwards Duke of Sully and a minister of Henry.

61. Vienna . . . Lucerne. Catholic centers of Austria and Switzerland, respectively.

63. Philip . . . Mexican pistoles. Philip II of Spain, champion of Catholicism and a loyal supporter of the League, was supplying his treasury with gold from the mines of Mexico. See the first stanza of the *Armada*. A pistole is a Spanish coin worth about four dollars.

THE BATTLE OF NASEBY

The Battle of Naseby. This battle (June 14, 1645) marked the end of the first civil war in England. It was the culmination of the struggle for the crown of England, with King Charles I at the head of the Royalists and Oliver Cromwell in command of the Parliamentary troops.

The story is told by a Puritan, the length of whose name is not an exaggeration.—**Ireton** was one of Cromwell's staunch commanders.

1. in triumph from the North. Less than a year prior to the Battle of Naseby, Cromwell's troops had defeated the Royalists at Marston Moor, in the north of England.

12. Astley. Sir Jacob (afterwards Lord) Astley was in command of the center division of the Royalist army.—**Sir Marmaduke.** Sir

Marmaduke Langdale had charge of the left wing of Charles's forces.—
Rupert of the Rhine. Prince Rupert of Bavaria was a nephew of
Charles, and commander of the right division of the King's troops in
this battle. He was a dashing cavalry leader whose forces had remained undefeated until Cromwell's own "Ironside" troops hurled
him back at Marston Moor.

22. **bravoes of Alsatia.** The German troops of Rupert.—**Whitehall.**
The royal palace in London.

38. **Temple Bar.** A gateway in front of the Temple in London,
on which the heads of famous criminals were publicly exposed.

52. **diamonds and your spades.** Card playing was especially
offensive to the Puritans.

55. **Oxford halls.** King Charles had established his headquarters
in Oxford. The University was noted for its loyalty to the King.
—**Durham's stalls.** Durham cathedral was the seat of the
bishop, hence a Royalist center.

THE ARMADA

Armada. In July, 1588, the "Invincible Armada" of Spain, numbering almost 150 ships and bearing 22,000 soldiers, appeared off the
coast of England. To repel this invasion the English fleet had but
60 available ships, and a land force of raw recruits, hurriedly called
together, under the command of the inefficient Leicester. Lord Charles
Howard, Lord High Admiral of England, adopted the policy of pursuing the Armada, and cutting off straggling vessels. Finally, in a
running battle off Calais, the Spaniards were badly defeated and
driven northward. The English fleet followed, and harassed the enemy, as far as the Firth of Forth. Then a great storm set in, almost
completing the destruction of the Armada, so that fewer than half
of the ships and men returned to Spain three months later. Read
Kingsley's *Westward Ho!* for a vivid account of the battle.

10. **tall Pinta.** The vessels of the Armada rode high out of the
water, hence their clumsiness.

21-22. **Lion of the sea . . . gay lilies down.** A reference to the design on the British flag. The lion symbolizes England; the lilies, France.

23-24. Picard field, etc. The Battle of Crecy (1346), in Picardy, in which Edward III of England overwhelmingly defeated the French forces under Philip VI. Supporting Philip were the troops of the aged King of **Bohemia,** who was slain; **Genoese crossbowmen;** and the King of Bohemia's son, King of the Romans, hence heir to **Cæsar's shield.**

25. Agincourt. At Agincourt, near Crecy, in 1415, Henry V overthrew the French army, composed chiefly of knights.

30. semper eadem. "Always the same." This motto was inscribed on the English banner.

35. From Eddystone . . . to Milford Bay. From one end of England to the other. See any map of England for the location of these places.

41. Tamar's glittering waves. Tamar River is in southwestern England, forming a part of the boundary line between Devon and Cornwall.

42. Mendip's sunless caves. The mines in the Mendip Hills, southwest of Bristol.

43. Longleat's towers. A country mansion near Salisbury.—**Cranbourne's oaks.** Cranborn Chase, an ancient forest in the shires of Dorset and Wilts.

44. Stonehenge. Two concentric circles of upright stones, eight miles north of Salisbury, presumably the remains of a temple of the Druids.—**Beaulieu.** A village near Southampton.

65. Darwin's rocky dales. Probably Darwen, a parliamentary division in northeastern Lancashire.

67. Malvern's lonely height. Probably Worcester Beacon, one of the hills in the Malvern range, near Gloucester.

68. Wrekin's crest. The Wrekin is a hill in Shropshire, near Wellington.

69. Ely's stately fane. The cathedral of Ely, a town fifteen miles from Cambridge.

73. Gaunt's embattled pile. Lancaster castle, once the stronghold of the Duke of Gaunt.

ECLECTIC ENGLISH CLASSICS

New Edition in Cloth. The 20 Cent Series
53 Volumes, including the following:

Addison's Sir Roger de Coverley Papers (Underwood)	$0.20
Arnold's Sohrab and Rustum (Tanner)	.20
Burke's Conciliation with the American Colonies (Clark)	.20
Byron's Childe Harold (Canto IV), Prisoner of Chillon, Mazeppa, and other Selections (Venable)	.20
Carlyle's Essay on Burns (Miller)	.20
Coleridge's Ancient Mariner (Garrigues)	.20
Defoe's Robinson Crusoe (Stephens)	.20
Dickens's Tale of Two Cities (Pearce). Double number	.40
Franklin's Autobiography (Reid)	.20
George Eliot's Silas Marner (McKitrick)	.20
Goldsmith's Vicar of Wakefield (Hansen)	20
Gray's Elegy in a Country Churchyard, and Goldsmith's Deserted Village (Van Dyke)	.20
Irving's Sketch Book — Selections (St. John)	.20
Lincoln, Selections from	.20
Macaulay's Essays on Lord Clive and Warren Hastings (Holmes) Double number	.40
Lays of Ancient Rome (Atkinson)	.20
Life of Johnson (Lucas)	.20
Milton's Minor Poems (Buck)	.20
Old Testament Narratives (Baldwin)	.20
Pope's Rape of the Lock, and Essay on Man (Van Dyke)	.20
Scott's Ivanhoe (Schreiber). Double number	.40
Lady of the Lake (Bacon)	.20
Quentin Durward (Norris). Double number	.40
Shakespeare's As You Like It (North)	.20
Julius Caesar (Baker)	.20
Macbeth (Livengood)	.20
Merchant of Venice (Blakely)	.20
Midsummer-Night's Dream (Haney)	.20
Twelfth Night (Weld)	.20
Stevenson's Treasure Island (Fairley)	.20
Tennyson's Idylls of the King. Selections (Willard)	.20
Princess (Shryock)	.20
Thackeray's Henry Esmond (Bissell). Triple number	.60
Washington's Farewell Address, and Webster's First Bunker Hill Oration (Lewis)	.20

AMERICAN BOOK COMPANY

A HISTORY OF ENGLISH LITERATURE

By REUBEN POST HALLECK, M.A. (Yale), Louisville Male High School. Price, $1.25

HALLECK'S HISTORY OF ENGLISH LITERATURE traces the development of that literature from the earliest times to the present in a concise, interesting, and stimulating manner. Although the subject is presented so clearly that it can be readily comprehended by high school pupils, the treatment is sufficiently philosophic and suggestive for any student beginning the study.

¶ The book is a history of literature, and not a mere collection of biographical sketches. Only enough of the facts of an author's life are given to make students interested in him as a personality, and to show how his environment affected his work. Each author's productions, their relations to the age, and the reasons why they hold a position in literature, receive adequate treatment.

¶ One of the most striking features of the work consists in the way in which literary movements are clearly outlined at the beginning of each chapter. Special attention is given to the essential qualities which differentiate one period from another, and to the animating spirit of each age. The author shows that each period has contributed something definite to the literature of England.

¶ At the end of each chapter a carefully prepared list of books is given to direct the student in studying the original works of the authors treated. He is told not only what to read, but also where to find it at the least cost. The book contains a special literary map of England in colors.

AMERICAN BOOK COMPANY

A HISTORY OF AMERICAN LITERATURE

By REUBEN POST HALLECK, M.A.,
Principal, Male High School, Louisville, Ky.

$1.25

A COMPANION volume to the author's History of English Literature. It describes the greatest achievements in American literature from colonial times to the present, placing emphasis not only upon men, but also upon literary movements, the causes of which are thoroughly investigated. Further, the relation of each period of American literature to the corresponding epoch of English literature has been carefully brought out—and each period is illuminated by a brief survey of its history.

¶ The seven chapters of the book treat in succession of Colonial Literature, The Emergence of a Nation (1754-1809), the New York Group, The New England Group, Southern Literature, Western Literature, and the Eastern Realists. To these are added a supplementary list of less important authors and their chief works, as well as A Glance Backward, which emphasizes in brief compass the most important truths taught by American literature.

¶ At the end of each chapter is a summary which helps to fix the period in mind by briefly reviewing the most significant achievements. This is followed by extensive historical and literary references for further study, by a very helpful list of suggested readings, and by questions and suggestions, designed to stimulate the student's interest and enthusiasm, and to lead him to study and investigate further for himself the remarkable literary record of American aspiration and accomplishment.

AMERICAN BOOK COMPANY

(S.318)

COMPOSITION-RHETORIC

By STRATTON D. BROOKS, Superintendent of Schools, Boston, Mass., and MARIETTA HUBBARD, formerly English Department, High School, La Salle, Ill. Price, $1.00

THE fundamental aim of this volume is to enable pupils to express their thoughts freely, clearly, and forcibly.

At the same time it is designed to cultivate literary appreciation, and to develop some knowledge of rhetorical theory. The work follows closely the requirements of the College Entrance Examination Board, and of the New York State Education Department.

¶ In Part One are given the elements of description, narration, exposition, and argument; also special chapters on letter-writing and poetry. A more complete and comprehensive treatment of the four forms of discourse already discussed is furnished in Part Two. In each part is presented a series of themes covering these subjects, the purpose being to give the pupil inspiration, and that confidence in himself which comes from the frequent repetition of an act. A single new principle is introduced into each theme, and this is developed in the text, and illustrated by carefully selected examples.

¶ The pupils are taught how to correct their own errors, and also how to get the main thought in preparing their lessons. Careful coördination with the study of literature and with other school studies is made throughout the book.

¶ The modern character of the illustrative extracts can not fail to interest every boy and girl. Concise summaries are given following the treatment of the various forms of discourse, and toward the end of the book there is a very comprehensive and compact summary of grammatical principles. More than usual attention is devoted to the treatment of argument.

AMERICAN BOOK COMPANY
(S. 85)

WEBSTER'S DICTIONARIES

The Only Genuine School Editions

THESE Dictionaries are the acknowledged authority throughout the English-speaking world, and constitute a complete and progressive series, carefully graded, and adapted for all classes.

WEBSTER'S PRIMARY SCHOOL DICTIONARY $0.48

    Containing over 20,000 words and meanings, with over 400 illustrations.

WEBSTER'S COMMON SCHOOL DICTIONARY $0.72

    Containing over 25,000 words and meanings, with over 500 illustrations.

WEBSTER'S HIGH SCHOOL DICTIONARY $0.98

    Containing about 37,000 words and definitions, and an appendix giving a pronouncing vocabulary of Biblical, Classical, Mythological, Historical, and Geographical proper names, with over 800 illustrations.

WEBSTER'S ACADEMIC DICTIONARY
    Cloth, $1.50; Indexed $1.80
    Half Calf, $2.75; Indexed 3.00

    Abridged directly from the International Dictionary, and giving the orthography, pronunciation, definitions, and synonyms of about 60,000 words in common use, with an appendix containing various useful tables, and over 800 illustrations.

AMERICAN BOOK COMPANY
(S.104)

THE MASTERY OF BOOKS
By HARRY LYMAN KOOPMAN, A.M., Librarian
of Brown University.   Price, 90 cents

IN this book Mr. Koopman, whose experience and reputation as a librarian give him unusual qualifications as an adviser, presents to the student at the outset the advantages of reading, and the great field of literature open to the reader's choice. He takes counsel with the student as to his purpose, capacities, and opportunities in reading, and aims to assist him in following such methods and in turning to such classes of books as will further the attainment of his object.

¶ Pains are taken to provide the young student from the beginning with a knowledge, often lacking in older readers, of the simplest literary tools—reference books and catalogues. An entire chapter is given to the discussion of the nature and value of that form of printed matter which forms the chief reading of the modern world—periodical literature. Methods of note-taking and of mnemonics are fully described; and a highly suggestive and valuable chapter is devoted to larguage study.

¶ One of the most valuable chapters in the volume to most readers is that concerning courses of reading. In accordance with the author's new plan for the guidance of readers, a classified list of about fifteen hundred books is given, comprising the most valuable works in reference books, periodicals, philosophy, religion, mythology and folk-lore, biography, history, travels, sociology, natural sciences, art, poetry, fiction, Greek, Latin, and modern literatures. The latest and best editions are specified, and the relative value of the several works mentioned is indicated in notes.

AMERICAN BOOK COMPANY
(S. 106)

MASTERPIECES OF THE ENGLISH DRAMA

Edited under the supervision of FELIX E. SCHELLING, Ph.D., LL.D., Professor of History and English Literature, University of Pennsylvania.

Marlowe (Phelps)	Middleton (Sampson)
Chapman (Ellis)	Massinger (Sherman)
Beaumont and Fletcher (Schelling)	Webster and Tourneur (Thorndike)
Jonson (Rhys)	Congreve (Archer)
Goldsmith and Sheridan (Demmon)	

Each, 70 cents

THIS series presents the principal dramatists, covering English dramatic history from Marlowe's Tamburlaine in 1587 to Sheridan's School for Scandal in 1777. Each volume contains four or five plays, selected with reference to their actual worth and general interest, and also because they represent the best efforts of their authors in the different varieties of dramas chosen.

¶ The texts follow the authoritative old editions, but with such occasional departures as the results of recent critical scholarship demand. Spelling and punctuation have been modernized, and obsolete and occasional words referred to the glossaries. This makes the volumes suitable for the average reader as well as for the advanced scholar.

¶ Each volume is furnished with an introduction by a British or an American scholar of rank dealing with the dramatist and his work. Each volume contains a brief biographical note, and each play is preceded by an historical note, its source, date of composition, and other kindred matters. Adequate notes are furnished at the end.

AMERICAN BOOK COMPANY

(S. 100)

DESCRIPTIVE CATALOGUE OF HIGH SCHOOL AND COLLEGE TEXTBOOKS

Published Complete and in Sections

WE issue a Catalogue of High School and College Textbooks, which we have tried to make as valuable and as useful to teachers as possible. In this catalogue are set forth briefly and clearly the scope and leading characteristics of each of our best textbooks. In most cases there are also given testimonials from well-known teachers, which have been selected quite as much for their descriptive qualities as for their value as commendations.

¶ For the convenience of teachers this Catalogue is also published in separate sections treating of the various branches of study. These pamphlets are entitled · English, Mathematics, History and Political Science, Science, Modern Foreign Languages, Ancient Languages, Commercial Subjects and Philosophy and Education. A separate pamphlet is devoted to the Newest Books in all subjects.

¶ Teachers seeking the newest and best books for their classes are invited to send for any of these.

¶ Copies of our price lists, or of special circulars, in which these books are described at greater length than the space limitations of the catalogue permit, will be mailed to any address on request. Address all correspondence to the nearest office of the company.

AMERICAN BOOK COMPANY
(S.312)